A Pocket Book on
Potatoes

The vegetable that makes a meal

Rhona Newman

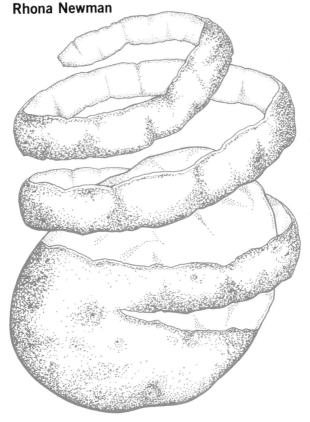

Octopus Books

Contents

First published 1984 by
Octopus Books Limited
59 Grosvenor Street
London W1

© 1984 Octopus Books Limited

ISBN 0 7064 2070 5

Produced by Mandarin Publishers Ltd
22a Westlands Road, Quarry Bay,
Hong Kong

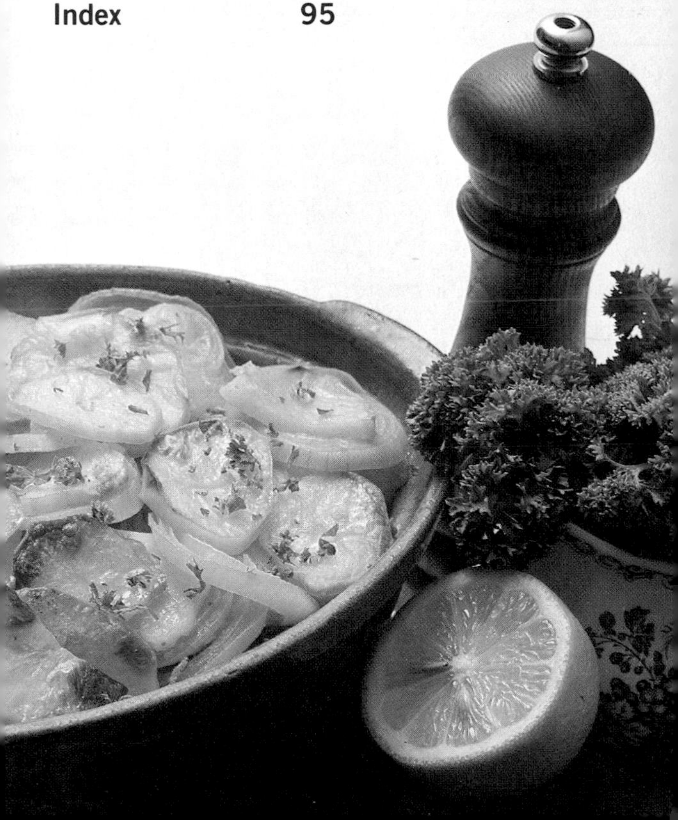

Introduction

The potato is a perennial herb which belongs to the plant family *Solanaceae.* It is grown for the edible tubers which form as swellings on the tips of the underground stems.

Potatoes are now one of the world's most important foods. Many varieties are produced, and quality and production have much improved since the arrival of the potato in Great Britain during the sixteenth century. Potatoes have since become very much a part of the British diet. An average of 102 kg/225 lb per person is consumed each year. A more positive attitude towards the value of potatoes in the diet has now been adopted, dismissing the idea that they are just a 'filler' and consequently fattening.

History

Potatoes had been grown in South America by the Incas for 2,000 years before they were discovered in Peru by the Spaniards during the sixteenth century. It is not known exactly who brought them to Britain, but legend has associated Raleigh and Drake with this. It is possible that Drake brought them as a ship store and discovered their food value because they kept the seamen healthy and free from scurvy during the voyage.

Such a vegetable was much needed in Britain in the sixteenth century as many people suffered from scurvy each winter. Initially, potatoes were only grown as a novelty in Britain, many people regarding them with suspicion, but during Charles II's reign, in the seventeenth century, it was suggested that potatoes should be planted throughout Britain to avoid famine. The suspicions remained, however, and it was only at the end of the eighteenth century that the useful contribution the potato made to the diet was finally recognised. Potatoes are cheap, versatile and nutritious. Many factors affect the nutritional content of the potato, but basically they are a useful source of protein, calcium, iron, vitamins B and C, and dietary fibre.

Helpful Hint
Store potatoes in a cool, dark, dry place. Warmth will cause sprouting, damp causes rot and light turns potatoes green. Do not store potatoes in polythene bags, condensation will form and cause rot.

Potato production

Today the production and processing of potatoes is a very big, efficient industry playing an important part in the country's economy. The Potato Marketing Board represents over 25,000 producers in Great Britain. It ensures that potatoes reaching the consumer are of the highest standard and that distribution is correctly organized throughout the country.

In a normal season over 6 million tonnes of potatoes are harvested. These may be used for seed tubers, bought by domestic consumers, used in the catering industry, or used by the food-processing industry to meet the growing demand for prepared potato products such as crisps, instant potato mix, chips and croquettes. This reflects a more adventurous palate and busier life-style.

Nutritional value

Potatoes are recognized by nutritionists and dietitians as an important source of essential nutrients. Their importance in the diet varies with the amount of potato consumed, the daily average being about 175 g/6 oz. However, people on a limited budget tend to consume a larger quantity which makes the potato an important staple food for them.

The composition of the potato depends upon variety, climate, soil, fertilizers and environmental factors, but the nutritional content remains more or less the same.

Carbohydrate and protein

Potatoes are considered by many to be no more than a 'filler' or energy food and it is true that they consist of a large proportion of carbohydrate in the form of starch. However, it is important to remember that carbohydrate foods play an invaluable role in our diets as they are our bodies' main source of energy. If carbohydrates are omitted from the diet, expensive protein foods will be used to supply energy before being used for more vital processes like body repair. A useful amount of protein is found in potatoes, their contribution providing 3-4% of an average household total protein intake.

Minerals

Potatoes contain small amounts of many minerals, but they are quite an important source of iron and calcium. Iron is needed by the body for healthy blood, and calcium for healthy bones, teeth, muscles and the clotting of blood.

Vitamins

Vitamins are also to be found in potatoes, notably the B vitamins and vitamin C. The B vitamins are essential for the body to utilize carbohydrate for energy, maintaining the health of the heart, nervous system, digestive system and skin. Potatoes are a particularly good source of vitamin B_1. Vitamin C helps to increase resistance to infection and keeps gums, muscles, bones and skin healthy. It may also help to prevent the build-up of cholesterol in the arteries, and therefore lessen the likelihood of heart attacks.

Helpful Hints

Whenever possible, serve potatoes with their skins on. Many of the minerals and vitamins in a potato are situated just below the skin and are quickly lost if the potato is peeled before cooking.

Cook potatoes in a minimum amount of water to minimize the loss of nutrients and simmer them gently to prevent the potatoes from breaking up. Cut the potatoes to a uniform size if necessary to ensure even cooking.

Three medium boiled potatoes, about 250 g/8 oz, provides 185 Calories, the same weight of bread provides 570 — more than double the Calories.

As vitamins B and C are not stored by the body it is important that they are taken in the diet every day. As potatoes are consumed in quite large quantities each day they are a valuable source of these vitamins, particularly vitamin C. However, it should be noted that the vitamin C content decreases with the maturity of the potato and with storage. An old potato bought at the end of the year contains far less vitamin C than a new potato. Vitamin C can also be lost through cooking and by keeping cooked potatoes warm for long periods.

Potato Croquettes, page 24; Duchesse Potatoes, page 23; Chips, page 30; Baked Potatoes, page 26

Composition of potatoes

Protein	2%
Fat	0%
Carbohydrate	18%
Water	80%

Diet allergies

Unlike wheat and some cereal products, potatoes are not known to be the cause of any common allergy. If wheat cannot be included in the diet, potatoes can be used as an alternative thickening agent or 'filler' food. Those with allergies to dairy produce can eat potatoes provided no butter, cream nor milk are added to them.

Potatoes and dietary fibre

Dietary fibre is the residue of plant cell walls in fruit, vegetables and cereals. It consists mainly of cellulose, which is not actually absorbed by our bodies – the reason dietary fibre has not been considered essential in the past. Fibre absorbs water, and its main function is to increase the bulk of the food in the intestines. This speeds up the passage of food through the digestive system, thereby preventing constipation and a build-up of harmful chemicals.

With increasing affluence the Western diet has become much refined and this fibre has been removed from processed foods. The loss of fibre has now been linked with the increase in digestive and heart diseases. In Third World countries and rural areas of the Western World, where foods are unrefined and fibre intake is higher, there is a lower incidence of these diseases. As a nation, the UK's intake of dietary fibre is low, but nutritional authorities are now urging a general increase to try to reduce the incidence of related diseases.

The potato is a useful source of fibre, particularly if the skin is eaten as in baked and sometimes boiled potatoes.

Potatoes and slimming

As they are mainly a carbohydrate food, potatoes are thought by many people to be high in calories and fattening. Many slimming diets in the past were based on a low-carbohydrate intake, and potatoes were eliminated from the diet programme. Like other vegetables, potatoes contain a large proportion of water – about 75-80% as opposed to bread, containing about 40%. Thus, weight for weight, potatoes contain far fewer calories than bread. Potatoes actually contribute less than 10% of our total carbohydrate intake.

Any food will be fattening if eaten in excess. Furthermore, it is now realized that it is the fats in the diet that cause more problems to health and weight. Fats have double the energy value of carbohydrates, so it is these which should be omitted from the diet.

Recent research has shown that foods which are high in

fibre (see opposite), are useful in a slimming diet and the trend now is towards high-carbohydrate diets. Fibrous foods need lots of chewing, which can slow down eating and should result in the dieter eating less before the feeling of fullness is achieved. As fibre absorbs and holds water it swells to a greater bulk in the stomach and also helps to give the feeling of fullness. On a high-fibre diet slimmers find that they are satisfied on three meals a day which is not usually the case on a low carbohydrate diet.

Baked potatoes are particularly useful as part of a slimming diet as they can be served as a main course with a variety of low-calorie fillings. Any form of potato can be included in a diet programme provided they are not cooked in oil or fat or served with lashings of butter and cream, nor eaten in excess – this is when they become a 'fattening' food as you can see from the chart below.

Energy value per 100 g/3½ oz potato

Cooking method	Raw	Boiled	Chips	Roast
kJ	318	331	989	515
Cal	76	79	236	123

Potatoes and teeth

Dental decay is associated with carbohydrates, both in the form of starch and sugars. All carbohydrates are converted to sugars during digestion, but it is the carbohydrate residue left in the mouth that can destroy teeth.

Research has shown that communities relying on cereals as a carbohydrate food have a higher incidence of dental caries than those eating a mainstay diet of potatoes. This could be because potatoes contain significant amounts of fluorine, a chemical that some local authorities add to the water, and that is added to toothpaste, in an attempt to reduce dental caries. It can also be given to children in drop or tablet form.

Another reason could be that boiled potatoes have been shown to give lower sugar levels in the saliva than cereal foodstuffs such as bread, wheat biscuits and pasta.

Buyer's guide

In the past, potatoes were rarely labelled in the shops, so the consumer did not know the type of potato they were buying. Recent EEC legislation stipulates that retailers are obliged to label all potatoes clearly with the name of the variety; this will help the consumer to recognize and get to know the different varieties.

The charts on pages 12 and 13 give information about the more common varieties found in the shops and their suitability for different cooking methods.

Varieties

Altogether over 200 varieties of potato are grown, but only about 50 of varying colour, flavour and texture are grown commercially for human consumption.

The potatoes are divided into two groups, the earlies or new potatoes and the maincrop varieties. Here are some of the most common ones:

Earlies	**Maincrop**
Home Guard	Desirée
Maris Pear	King Edward
Pentland Javelin	Maris Piper
Ulster Sceptre	Pentland Crown
Wilja	Pentland Dell
Epicure	Pentland Hawk
Maris Bard	Pentland Ivory
Estima	Pentland Squire
Ulster Prince	Record
Craig's Alliance	
Peel Craig's Royal	
Annan Comet	

Earlies

The earlies are harvested from late May and early June. They are immature tubers with a flaky skin and are particularly suitable for boiling, steaming and using in salads. They have an excellent flavour and firm, waxy texture. The larger potatoes can be cut and used to make chips. Buy new potatoes in small quantities and use quickly to make the most of their flavour.

Maincrop

The maincrop potatoes are harvested in September and October as they require a longer growing period to become mature. Once harvested, maincrop potatoes are stored in a controlled environment and are sold off throughout the winter until the following May. Maincrop potatoes have a firm, waxy flesh in the autumn, but this becomes more floury during storage. Despite a gradual loss of vitamin C, they can still make a useful contribution to the diet.

Although maincrop potatoes do not have quite as good a flavour as the earlies they are more flexible in cooking.

Seed potatoes

Seed potatoes for the following year's crop are mostly grown in the cooler climate of Scotland. They conform to strict health regulations designed to prevent the spread of disease.

Buying and storing potatoes

In general, choose potatoes which are a good shape, have shallow eyes and undamaged skins. Greening occurs if the potatoes have been exposed to light and it should be removed before cooking. Small amounts of green potato are quite harmless, but large quantities are poisonous. Very dirty potatoes are not a good buy.

Open markets and stalls are more likely to have a lower standard of potatoes, so it is often worth buying potatoes from a reputable greengrocer or supermarket, where potatoes are usually graded to a higher standard. Any extra cost is worth it in terms of easier preparation and less wastage.

Maincrop potatoes are available from August onwards and unlike new potatoes it may be worth buying them in bulk. Many wholesalers and greengrocers will deliver large quantities on a weekly or monthly basis. This ensures that you always have potatoes in the kitchen and saves carrying them from the shops.

Keep potatoes in brown paper packs, if possible, to keep out light, and store in a cool, dry, dark place. The best temperature is 5-10°C (40-50°F). A garage, shed or cellar is usually ideal.

British early potatoes

Potato	Description	Boiled	Mashed	Jacket	Roast	Chips or sauté	Salads
Home Guard	Creamy white flesh. Good cooking quality, particularly in the early season. Tendency to blacken after cooking later in season. Not as waxy as some earlies – soft, slightly dry texture.	●●●●	–	–	●●	●●	●●●
Maris Peer	Creamy white flesh. Good cooking quality. Rarely disintegrates during cooking. Moderately waxy texture and slightly dry.	●●●●	–	■	●●●	●●●	●●●
Pentland Javelin	A very white-fleshed potato with good shape. Good cooking quality. Moderately waxy.	●●●	–	–	●●	●●	●●●
Ulster Sceptre	White flesh. Good cooking quality. Rarely discolours. Moderately soft, waxy texture. One of the first earlies available in shops.	●●●	–	–	●●	●●●	●●●
Wilja	Pale yellow-fleshed potato. Good cooking quality. Rarely disintegrates. Moderately soft, slightly dry texture. Not as waxy as some earlies.	●●●	–	■	●●	●●●	●●●

Other earlies with similar cooking qualities are: Epicure, Maris Bard, Estima, Ulster Prince, Craig's Alliance, Annan Comet. The red Craig's Alliance has a distinctive pink skin.

Key   Can be used ●   Good ●●   Very good ●●●   Excellent ●●●●

Suitable from August ■
– Not suitable

British maincrop potatoes

Potato	Description	Boiled	Mashed	Jacket	Roast	Chips or sauté	Salads
Desirée	Pink skin with yellow flesh. Good cooking quality. Rarely disintegrates. Variable shape, moderately soft texture and not too dry.	●●●	●●	●●●	●●●	●●●●●	●
King Edward	Particularly pink skin with creamy flesh. Rarely discolours. Soft, dry, floury texture. High-quality potato for domestic use.	●●●●	●●	●●●	●●●●	●●●●	●
Maris Piper	Creamy white flesh. Good cooking quality. Rarely discolours. Soft, dry, floury texture. Attractive, uniformly shaped tubers.	●●●	●●●	●●●	●●●●	●●●●●	●
Pentland Crown	Creamy white flesh. Moderate cooking quality. Moderately soft with a tendency to wetness.	●●	●	●●●	●●	●	–
Pentland Dell	White to cream flesh. Moderate cooking quality. Tendency to disintegrate during cooking. Soft, dry texture. Oval-shaped potato.	●●	●	●●●	●●	●	●
Pentland Hawk	Cream flesh. Moderate cooking quality. Firm, slightly dry texture.	●●●	●●	●●●	●	●	●

Other maincrop potatoes grown in quite large quantities are the Pentland Ivory, which has good all-round cooking qualities but a tendency to blacken after cooking; and Pentland Squire, which is a good all-rounder with a soft, dry texture. Record Variety is used almost entirely in the processing industry.

Potato processing

This is rapidly becoming a big industry and there is a wide variety of dried and frozen potato products on the market. Although they are more expensive than the raw vegetable, they require little if any further preparation, there is no waste and they can be used in the same ways as fresh potatoes.

Instant potato

There are several types available, some in powder form and some in granules. It is pre-cooked dehydrated potato from which only water has been removed. Some manufacturers add extra vitamin C which makes it more nutritious than fresh potatoes and some add dried milk and butter for flavour. To serve, you simply add hot water. Extra milk, butter, plus other flavouring can be beaten in. Use in place of mashed potato.

Canned potatoes

Cans are filled with peeled new potatoes and brine and processed at high temperatures. They only require re-heating; no further cooking is needed. Canned potatoes are ideal to use in salads, as a garnish and for sautéing.

Potato crisps, sticks and snacks

There are many shapes and flavours of potato snack products on the supermarket shelves, but crisps still remain the most popular of all the potato products.

These are usually thought of as party nibbles, snacks and between-meal 'fillers', but they can be crushed and used as a crispy topping for savoury dishes or a coating for rissoles or fish cakes. They also make an excellent accompaniment to grilled or fried food.

Frozen prepared potatoes

There is an ever-increasing range of frozen potato products available in the shops.

Frozen chips Potatoes are cut into straight or crinkle-shaped chips, then frozen. They can be taken straight from the freezer and plunged immediately into a pan of hot fat to cook.

Oven chips Oven chips are becoming increasingly popular. They are shaped and partially cooked in hot oil before freezing. You cook them in a hot oven or under a grill so there is no hot fat to deal with and no frying odours or fumes. Because they are not fried in oil, cooked oven chips contain fewer calories than traditional chips.

Croquette potatoes These are creamy mashed potato shaped into croquettes and covered with crisp bread-crumbs. They can be cooked quickly from frozen in shallow or deep fat (see below), or they can be brushed with oil and cooked under the grill or baked in the oven.

Potato fritters Small slices of potato coated in batter. They can be fried, grilled or baked. The fat must be really hot to seal the fritters as soon as they are immersed in the pan. Serve with fried or grilled foods.

Potato waffles These are a novel way of serving potatoes and can be the base for savoury snacks, breakfast, party fare, or simply served as an accompaniment.

The waffles consist of creamy mashed potato which has been moulded in a waffle iron. They are then blanched in hot oil before freezing. Like oven chips, they can be grilled or baked as well as shallow or deep fat fried.

Potato Croquettes

Classic potato dishes

Many potato dishes are given their traditional French name in recipe books and on restaurant menus. These can throw both the novice cook and diner into total confusion so here is a description of the classic potato dishes.

Pommes Allumettes (see page 31) Small matchstick chips, also called Straw Potatoes.

Pommes Anna Wafer-thin sliced potatoes baked with butter in a large dish or individual dariole moulds (see page 89).

Pommes Annette A variation of Pommes Anna made with potatoes cut into julienne strips rather than slices.

Pommes Berny Croquette potato mixture shaped into balls then coated in egg and flaked almonds and deep fried.

Pommes au Beurre Boiled or steamed potatoes tossed with butter.

Pommes Boulangère Sliced potatoes baked with onions and stock (see page 88).

Pommes Byron Potato slices sprinkled with cream and grated cheese, baked until soft, then browned under the grill.

Pommes Chatouillard Long ribbons of potato deep fat fried until they puff and turn golden.

Pommes Croquette Puréed potato shaped into small barrels coated in egg and breadcrumbs and deep fried (see page 24).

Pommes Dauphine Croquette potato mixture mixed with half as much choux pastry, shaped into balls and deep fried until golden.

Pommes Delmonico Diced potatoes cooked in cream, then sprinkled with a mixture of breadcrumbs and cheese.

Pommes Farçies Any form of stuffed potato.

Pommes Fondantes Small even-sized potatoes sprinkled with salt and pepper, then half-covered with stock and baked in the oven.

Pommes Frites French fries or chips (see page 33).

Pommes Gaufrettes Lattice-shaped crisps (see page 32).

Pommes Gratinées Mashed potato sprinkled with cheese and browned.

Pommes Hongroise Potato slices mixed with a little sautéed onion, chopped tomato and beef stock then baked until tender.

Pommes Julienne Thin strips of potato fried in deep fat.

Pommes Lyonnaise Sliced sauté potatoes mixed with lightly fried onion rings.

Pommes Macaire The pulp from baked jacket potatoes mixed with butter and seasoning, shaped into a round and fried in shallow fat.

Pommes Marquise Duchesse potatoes with the addition of tomato purée.

Pommes Nouvelles New potatoes.

Pommes Parisienne Small balls of potato, parboiled and sautéed or roasted in the oven (see page 33).

Pommes Paysanne Large, diced potatoes sautéed in butter and flavoured with salt, pepper, sorrel, chervil and garlic.

Pommes Persillées Boiled or steamed potatoes coated in melted butter and sprinkled with plenty of freshly chopped parsley.

Pommes Polonaise New potatoes dressed with breadcrumbs, browned in butter and mixed with chopped parsley.

Pommes Purée or **Pommes Mousseline** Sieved mashed potatoes whipped with salt, pepper, butter and cream.

Pommes en Robe de Chambre Potatoes steamed in their jackets.

Pommes Sautées Sliced cooked potatoes fried in butter or oil and sprinkled with parsley (see page 32).

Pommes Soufflées Thinly sliced potatoes that are double fried in deep fat until they puff out and turn golden and crispy.

Salade Cressonière Potato salad with watercress, garnished with chopped parsley, chervil and sieved hard-boiled egg.

Salade Hongroise Potato salad dressed with lemon and oil and spiced with grated horseradish, shredded cabbage and thin strips of ham and bacon.

Salade Niçoise Equal portions of potatoes, French beans and tomato quarters in vinaigrette dressing, decorated with anchovy strips, olives and capers. Quartered hard-boiled eggs are usually added.

Basic Cooking Methods

The greatest advantage of the potato is its versatility in cooking. There are numerous ways of serving potatoes as an accompaniment to meat, fish or eggs, and they form part of many traditional British dishes such as 'bangers and mash', fish and chips, and roast meat and potatoes. As well as making an ideal accompaniment in itself, the simple boiled potato can be made into salads, or served hot tossed in flavoured butters.

Potatoes are an important ingredient in all kinds of dishes, whether as a topping, part of a dough, or a filling for a flan, pie, omelette or pancake. They can also be included in soups, loaves, savoury burgers, casseroles and even cakes and desserts.

BOILED POTATOES

Old potatoes
Preparation Old potatoes should be washed and thinly peeled if necessary, but to gain maximum nutritional value they should be cooked in their skins. The skins will slip off easily after cooking. Cut large potatoes so that all the pieces are of an even size.

To boil Place in a saucepan and cover with *cold water*. Add 1 teaspoon salt, if liked, for every 500 g/1 lb potatoes, cover and bring to the boil. Reduce the heat and cook gently for 20 to 30 minutes until the potatoes are just soft when pierced with a knife. Drain the potatoes, reserving the liquid for stock, gravy or soup, then return the potatoes to the pan and dry off by cooking over a gentle heat for 1 to 2 minutes.

To serve Serve boiled potatoes plain, or toss in butter and sprinkle with parsley or chives. Serve immediately.

Note: If using a variety of potato that tends to discolour during cooking, add 2 teaspoons vinegar or lemon juice to each 600 ml/1 pint (2½ cups) water.

New potatoes
Preparation Scrub the potatoes or scrape, if necessary, but preferably leave the skins on. Cut any larger potatoes so they are of uniform size.

To boil Bring a saucepan of water to the boil, adding a sprig of fresh mint and 1 teaspoon salt, if liked, for each

Duchesse Potatoes, page 23; Pommes Boulangère, page 88; Sauté Potatoes page 32

500 g/1 lb potatoes. Add the potatoes. (Putting them straight into boiling water helps to retain their flavour.) Cover the pan and return to the boil. Reduce the heat and cook gently for 15 to 20 minutes until they feel soft when pierced with a knife. The cooking time will vary according to the size of the potatoes. Drain the potatoes, reserving the liquid for stock, gravy or soup, then return the potatoes to the pan and dry off by cooking over a gentle heat.

To serve Turn into a warmed serving dish and serve tossed in butter and/or chopped herbs.

Steamed potatoes

Both old and new potatoes can be steamed instead of boiled, and more nutrients will be retained by this method. Steaming also prevents the potatoes from breaking up.

To steam Prepare the potatoes as for boiling and place in the perforated tier of a steamer or in a metal colander over a saucepan of boiling water. Cover and steam until they are just tender. Small new potatoes will take about 20 minutes, medium-sized old potatoes about 30 minutes.

Pressure-cooked potatoes

To save time, potatoes can be cooked in a pressure cooker, possibly with other root vegetables. However, it is important not to overcook vegetables and, as cookers vary, take care to follow instructions given in the manufacturer's handbook.

Boiled or steamed potato recipes

Many dishes incorporate boiled or steamed potatoes. The most common are salads, but sliced potatoes are often used as a topping or layered with savoury fillings.

Freezer note: Cooked dishes using boiled or steamed potatoes can be frozen for up to 3 months. To serve, reheat from frozen or thaw first. Plain boiled or steamed potatoes are not so successful when frozen.

French Dauphinois

Metric/Imperial	*American*
1 kg/2 lb potatoes, peeled	2 lb potatoes, peeled
25 g/1 oz butter	2 tablespoons butter
1 garlic clove, crushed	1 garlic clove, crushed
150 ml/¼ pint single cream	⅔ cup light cream
salt and pepper	salt and pepper
grated nutmeg	grated nutmeg
175 g/6 oz Cheddar cheese, grated	1½ cups grated Cheddar cheese

Thinly slice the potatoes and simmer in salted water for 3 to 5 minutes, then drain. Brush the bottom and sides of a large shallow ovenproof dish with a little melted butter. Mix together the garlic and cream.

Place a layer of potatoes in the dish, then sprinkle with salt, pepper and nutmeg. Dot with a little butter, sprinkle with some cheese and pour a little cream over. Repeat the layers, finishing with a layer of cheese and cream.

Cover with foil and place in a preheated moderate oven (180°C/350°F, Gas Mark 4) for 30 minutes or until the potatoes are tender. Brown under a preheated grill for 5 minutes until the cheese is bubbling and golden. Serve immediately. Serves 4-6.

New Potatoes Maître d'Hôtel

Metric/Imperial	American
750 g/1½ lb new potatoes	1½ lb new potatoes
50 g/2 oz butter	¼ cup butter
2 spring onions, finely chopped	2 scallions, finely chopped
chopped parsley	chopped parsley
salt and pepper	salt and pepper
4 tablespoons single cream	4 tablespoons light cream

Bring a saucepan of salted water to the boil, add the potatoes and cook for 15 to 20 minutes until just tender. Drain the potatoes, peel and cut into thick slices. Melt the butter in an ovenproof dish and place the potatoes in layers, sprinkling each one with onion (scallion), parsley, salt and pepper. Heat the cream until almost boiling and pour over the potatoes. Place in a preheated cool oven (150°C/300°F, Gas Mark 2) for 20 minutes or until the potatoes are heated through. Serves 4.

Basic Potato Salad

Metric/Imperial	American
500 g/1 lb new potatoes, boiled	1 lb new potatoes, boiled
150 ml/¼ pint mayonnaise	⅔ cup mayonnaise
salt and pepper	salt and pepper

Remove the skins from the potatoes and cut into dice. Place in a bowl with the mayonnaise, salt and pepper. Toss together and add herbs or vegetables, if liked. Serves 4.
Variations
Flavour basic potato salad with one or more of the following: chopped parsley; chopped mint; chopped chives; chopped green or red peppers; diced cucumber; sweetcorn (corn kernels); 1 tablespoon chutney; chopped spring onion (scallion); mixed cooked vegetables; chopped celery; sliced mushrooms; chopped tomatoes; chopped ham; chopped gherkins.
Note: Make a potato salad a few hours before serving to allow the flavours to develop.

MASHED POTATOES

It is only possible to mash old potatoes, so if mashed potatoes are required when only new ones are in season, use an instant potato mix.

To mash Prepare and cook potatoes as for serving boiled (see page 18). Drain the potatoes, then return to the saucepan. Place the pan over a gentle heat and mash thoroughly, preferably with a masher. Season and serve plain with a knob of butter, or use in a recipe as required.

To cream potatoes For each 500 g/1 lb potatoes, add 25-50 g/1-2 oz (2-4 tablespoons) butter or margarine and 2 tablespoons *hot* milk or cream. Never use cold milk or the potato will become tacky. Beat thoroughly with a wooden spoon until fluffy and white. Season to taste.

To serve Place mashed potato in a warmed serving dish. If liked, use a fork to create decorative swirls and sprinkle with parsley.

Variations

Mix mashed or creamed potato with any of the following: chopped chives or spring onions (scallions); grated cheese; chopped cooked spinach; cooked mashed swede (rutabaga); chopped mint; tomato sauce; curry powder fried in a little butter; grated nutmeg.

Helpful Hints

Mashed potato is often used as a topping for savoury dishes. To give a crisp brown finish, dot with butter and cheese, if liked, and place under a preheated grill for 5 minutes.

It is important that mashed potato that is to be piped is completely free of lumps. It should therefore be sieved or passed through a ricer after the initial mashing.

Freezer note: Plain mashed potato, not creamed, can successfully be frozen. Divide into suitably sized portions for the family requirements, and pack in plastic containers. Cover and freeze. To serve, thaw at room temperature, then reheat potato in a covered ovenproof dish in a preheated moderately hot oven (190°C/375°F, Gas Mark 5) for 25 to 30 minutes. When hot, beat in butter, milk and any additional flavouring or seasoning.

Duchesse Potatoes

Metric/Imperial	*American*
500 g/1 lb warm mashed and sieved potato	2 cups warm mashed and sieved potato
25 g/1 oz butter	2 tablespoons butter
1 egg yolk	1 egg yolk
salt and pepper	salt and pepper

Add the butter, egg yolk and salt and pepper to taste to the warm potato.

Beat well and place the mixture in a large strong piping (pastry) bag fitted with a Number 10 star nozzle. Pipe pyramids or swirls on to a greased baking sheet. Brush lightly with melted margarine.

Place under a preheated grill (broiler) or in a preheated moderately hot oven (200°C/400°F, Gas Mark 6) for 15 to 20 minutes. Serves 4.

Potato Waffles, page 25

Potato nests

Make up Duchesse potato mixture (see page 23), and place in a piping (pastry) bag fitted with a Number 10 star nozzle. Pipe into small nests on a greased baking sheet. Brush with melted margarine and place in a preheated moderately hot oven (200°C/400°F, Gas Mark 6) for 15 to 20 minutes. Fill the cavities with a hot savoury filling. Serve immediately garnished with parsley.

Freezer note: If Duchesse potatoes or Potato nests are to be frozen, cook in the oven for 10 minutes, then cool. Open freeze on a baking sheet until frozen, then pack into bags and seal.

To serve from the freezer, brush frozen Duchesse potatoes or Potato nests with beaten egg and place on a greased baking sheet. Reheat in a moderately hot oven (200°C/400°F, Gas Mark 6) for 30 minutes. Serve as above.

Potato Croquettes

Metric/Imperial	*American*
1 kg/2 lb Duchesse mixture	4 cups Duchesse mixture
25 g/1 oz plain flour	¼ cup all-purpose flour
1 egg, beaten	1 egg, beaten
125 g/4 oz dry breadcrumbs	1 cup dry bread crumbs
oil, for deep fat frying	oil, for deep fat frying

Cool the Duchesse mixture and mould into cork shapes. Toss lightly in the flour, then coat in beaten egg and breadcrumbs.

Heat the oil to 190°C/375°F, place the croquettes in the frying basket and lower into the fat. Fry a few at a time for 5 minutes until crisp and golden, drain and transfer to a warmed serving dish. Makes 6-8.

Variation

Caraway potato croquettes Follow the recipe for Croquettes, adding 1 teaspoon caraway seeds. Serve with pork fillet, grilled chicken, or veal.

Herb Croquettes Add 4 tablespoons finely chopped fresh herbs.

Helpful Hints

For really light results use hot milk when mashing or creaming potatoes.

Never attempt to freeze raw potatoes. However, most forms of cooked potato, and prepared dishes containing potatoes, can be frozen successfully.

Cooked or prepared dishes which include potato can also be frozen. Guidelines for preparing, packing and cooking frozen potato can be found throughout this section.

Potato Waffles

Potato waffles can be used as a base for many savoury toppings such as: grilled cheese and tomato; cooked sausages and bacon; cooked kidneys and mushrooms; baked beans; scrambled eggs.

Metric/Imperial	American
350 g/12 oz potatoes, boiled and mashed	¾ lb potatoes, boiled and mashed
salt and pepper	salt and pepper
2 eggs	2 eggs
4 tablespoons self-raising flour	4 tablespoons self-rising flour
1 tablespoon oil	1 tablespoon oil
150 ml/¼ pint milk	⅔ cup milk

Heat an electric waffle maker following the manufacturer's instructions.

Place the potato in a bowl and add salt and pepper to taste. Separate 1 egg and whisk the white until stiff. Whisk the yolk with the remaining egg, the flour and oil until smooth. Gradually whisk in the potato, then the milk to make a smooth, thick batter. Using a metal spoon, fold in the whisked egg white.

When the waffle maker has reached the correct temperature, brush the plates with oil. Pour about 3 tablespoons batter over the plates so they are just covered. Close the waffle maker and cook for 3½ to 4 minutes until browned. Serve immediately with butter. Makes 8.

BAKED POTATOES

During the nineteenth century and up to the First World War, baked potato stalls were a common sight in London and other cities. People would buy them as a snack or light meal just as a bag of chips or potato crisps might be bought today.

In recent years there has been a revival of the baked potato. Many pubs, restaurants and take-away outlets serve them with appetizing fillings.

Old Potatoes

Preparation Allow 1 potato per person. Choose old ones weighing 175-250g/6-8oz (½lb). Wash and scrub the potatoes well to remove the dirt. (It is possible to buy potatoes ready-prepared for baking from some shops.) Prick the skins with a fork or score with a knife. If soft skins are preferred, rub the potatoes with butter or margarine and wrap them individually in foil before baking.

To bake Place potatoes on the open shelf of a preheated moderately hot oven (200°C/400°F, Gas Mark 6) and bake for 1 hour, or longer for larger potatoes, until they 'give' when pressed.

To Serve

Collar baked: Cut a slice from the top of the baked potato. Scoop out the pulp and mash with a little butter, salt and pepper. Pile back into the skins, pushing the mixture to the side and up around the top to form a collar. Spoon a chosen filling into the centre.

Crossed: Make a large cross incision in the potato. Holding the potato in a cloth, squeeze the base until the incision opens out. Sprinkle with salt and pepper and add a little butter. Spoon in a chosen filling if desired.

Stuffed: Cut the potato in half lengthwise and scoop the flesh into a bowl. Add a little butter, salt and pepper, then mash and beat until smooth. Fold in a chosen filling and pile back into the skins. Return to a hot oven (220°C/425°F, Gas Mark 7) or place under a preheated grill for 5 minutes to heat through.

Freezer note: Whole baked potatoes do not freeze well, but

A selection of stuffed baked potatoes – see above and pages 28 and 29

stuffed baked potatoes do. Arrange the stuffed potato halves on a baking sheet and open freeze, then cover and seal. To serve from the freezer, unwrap the frozen stuffed potatoes and place on a baking sheet in a preheated moderately hot oven (190°C/375°F, Gas Mark 5) for 25 to 30 minutes.

Fillings
Here are some filling suggestions. Allow about 50 g/2 oz per potato. The varieties are endless: Cottage cheese and walnuts; soured cream and chives; grated cheese and chutney; cream cheese and chopped pineapple; Coleslaw in a cone of salami sausage; hard-boiled egg and chopped tomato; smoked mackerel and mayonnaise; chopped prawns, mayonnaise and cream; corned beef and baked beans; chopped cooked chicken, peanut butter and cream; curd cheese, chopped peppers and chives; chopped cooked meat and curried mayonnaise; salami, cucumber and soured cream; cream cheese with garlic and peeled prawns; natural yogurt with bacon rolls.

New Potatoes

New potatoes are not suitable for traditional baking but can be cooked in the oven if wrapped in foil parcels.

Preparation Wash new potatoes and cut in half or slice. Place in the centre of a large piece of foil. Dot with butter and sprinkle liberally with salt and pepper. Seal the parcel and place on a baking sheet.

To bake Place potatoes in a pre-heated moderate oven (180°C/350°F, Gas Mark 4) and bake for 1 hour.

To serve Transfer to a warmed serving dish and sprinkle with parsley.

Variations

To vary the flavour of the potatoes, try adding one or more of the following to the parcel: finely chopped onion; crushed garlic cloves; chopped mint; chopped chives; dried mixed herbs; rosemary sprigs.

Helpful Hint

The cooking time for baked potatoes can be reduced by placing the potatoes on a baker. The metal prongs help to conduct heat through the potato. Alternatively, bake the potatoes with a metal skewer pushed through each one.

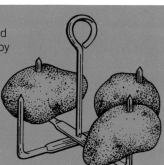

Sausage and Piccalilli Filling

Metric/Imperial	*American*
2 potatoes, baked in their jackets	2 potatoes, baked in their jackets
2 sausages, cooked and sliced	2 sausages, cooked and sliced
2 tablespoons piccalilli	2 tablespoons piccalilli
25 g/1 oz butter	2 tablespoons butter
salt and pepper	salt and pepper
1 tablespoon chopped fresh parsley	1 tablespoon chopped fresh parsley

Cut the baked potatoes in half and scoop out the flesh into
a bowl. Mix in the sausages, piccalilli, butter and plenty of
salt and pepper. Pile the mixture back into the skins then
sprinkle over chopped parsley. Serves 2.

Tuna and Onion Filling

Metric/Imperial	American
2 potatoes, baked in their jackets	2 potatoes, baked in their jackets
1 × 75 g/3 oz can tuna	1 × 3 oz can tuna
4 tablespoons mayonnaise	4 tablespoons mayonnaise
4 spring onions, trimmed and chopped	4 scallions, trimmed and chopped
grated rind of 1 small lemon	grated rind of 1 small lemon
salt and pepper	salt and pepper

Cut the baked potatoes in half and scoop out the flesh into
a bowl. Trim and chop the spring onions. Mix them into the
potato flesh with the drained tuna fish, mayonnaise, grated
lemon rind, and salt and pepper to taste. Pile the filling
back into the potato shells and brown them under a
preheated grill (broiler). Serves 2.

Mushroom and Cheese Filling

Metric/Imperial	American
2 potatoes, baked in their jackets	2 potatoes, baked in their jackets
100 g/4 oz button mushrooms, chopped	1 cup button mushrooms, chopped
25 g/1 oz butter	2 tablespoons butter
75 g/3 oz Cheddar cheese, grated	3/4 cup grated Cheddar cheese
salt and pepper	salt and pepper

Cut the baked potatoes in half and scoop the flesh into a
bowl. Fry the mushrooms in the butter until tender. Mix in
50 g/2 oz of the cheese with plenty of salt and pepper and
stir into the potato flesh. Return the filling to the shells,
sprinkle over the rest of the cheese and brown under a
preheated grill (broiler). Serves 2.

FRIED POTATOES

The fried forms of potato are always popular. Chips should be served with deep-fried foods, grills and some salad dishes. Straw potatoes, a smaller version of chips, are served as a garnish for grilled meats or roast poultry. Game chips or crisps should be served as an accompaniment to roast poultry or game, or as a garnish for grilled meats.

Chips, Straw Potatoes and Crinkle-cut Chips

Chips

Preparation Peel old potatoes and cut into slices and then fingers. The standard size is about 1 cm/½ inch) thick. Rinse well under cold running water or place in a bowl of iced water for 10 minutes to remove any excess starch. Drain and dry thoroughly on kitchen paper towels.

To fry Fill a deep fat pan with vegetable oil, lard or solid vegetable fats, to about a third full. Allow 900 ml/1½ pints (3¾ cups) oil for each 250 g/8 oz (½ lb) chips and never fill the pan more than two-thirds full with oil. Heat the oil to 190°C/375°F or until a small cube of bread will brown in 30 seconds.

Place a small quantity of chips in the frying basket and lower into the fat. Cook for 3 minutes, then remove the basket and allow the fat to reheat to the above temperature. Replace the basket in the fat and cook the chips for a further 5 minutes until crisp and golden brown.

To serve Drain well on kitchen paper towels and place in a warmed serving dish. Do not cover. Serve immediately. If kept warm for too long before serving the chips will become soft.

Freezer note: Prepare as above and cook in fat for 3 minutes. Drain on kitchen paper towels and allow to cool. Pack into polythene bags and seal, then freeze. To serve from the freezer, heat oil or fat to 190°C/375°F and fry frozen chips for 5 minutes. Drain and serve.

Straw Potatoes

Also known as matchstick potatoes, these are made in the same way as chips, but the potatoes are cut into far smaller even-sized straws. Care must be taken not to overcook them; the total frying time should be about 3 minutes. Fry and freeze as for chips.

Game Chips (crisps)

Preparation Peel medium or small old potatoes and slice thinly crosswise with a sharp knife, mandolin or the slicing blade of a food processor. Soak the potatoes in iced water for 15 to 20 minutes to remove excess starch and to crisp. Drain and dry thoroughly on a clean cloth or kitchen paper towels.

To fry Heat oil or fat to 190°C/375°F, place a few potato slices in the frying basket and lower into the fat. Cook for 2 to 4 minutes until the chips are golden brown, turning if necessary. Remove the basket and drain the chips on a cloth or paper towels. Repeat with the remaining potato slices.

To serve Serve in a bowl, sprinkled with salt. Not suitable for freezing.

Pommes Gaufrettes

These are similar to game chips but are cut into lattice shapes, which may require a little practice at first.

Preparation Choose medium old potatoes and peel thinly. Slice by reverse turns on the corrugated edge of a mandolin into thin lattice shapes. Alternatively use a corrugated potato slicer, but this method takes a great deal of skill and patience. Place in a bowl of iced water for 20 minutes, then drain and dry thoroughly.

To fry Heat oil or fat in a deep fat pan to 190°C/375°F. Place a few gaufrettes in the frying basket and lower into the fat. Cook for 2 to 4 minutes or until golden brown. Repeat until all the gaufrettes are cooked.

To serve Drain well on kitchen paper towels and serve hot, sprinkled with salt. Not suitable for freezing.

Sauté Potatoes

Old potatoes are best as they are more floury, but new ones can be sautéed. Use a heavy-based pan as this will distribute the heat evenly and allow the food to brown thoroughly during the brisk cooking.

Preparation Boil or steam the potatoes, drain and slice thickly.

To sauté For each 500 g/1 lb potatoes, heat 2 tablespoons oil and 25 g/1 oz (2 tablespoons) butter in a large frying pan (skillet). Add the potatoes and cook for about 10 minutes, turning often, until golden brown on both sides.

To serve Drain thoroughly on kitchen paper towels and place in a warmed serving dish. Sprinkle with salt and chopped parsley and serve with cold meat, poultry, grills or egg dishes. Not suitable for freezing.

Variations

Lyonnaise Potatoes Prepare as for Sauté Potatoes but add 1 chopped onion for each 500 g/1 lb potatoes. Sauté together, drain and serve sprinkled with chopped parsley.

Rosemary and Garlic Sauté Potatoes Sauté 1 crushed garlic clove and 1-2 tablespoons fresh rosemary leaves with each 500 g/1 lb potatoes. Serve sprinkled with freshly ground black pepper. These are particularly good served with lamb dishes.

Parisienne Potatoes

Preparation Choose old potatoes and peel thinly. Cut out balls with a small ball scoop (parisienne cutter).

To cook For each 500 g/1 lb potatoes, heat 2 tablespoons oil in a frying pan. Fry the potato balls for 10 minutes, then drain off any surplus fat. Transfer the balls to a roasting pan and complete the cooking in a preheated moderately hot oven (190°C/375°F, Gas Mark 5) for 30 minutes or until golden brown.

To serve Place in a warmed serving dish and toss in a little stock and butter. Garnish with parsley.

Variation

Parboil the potato balls gently, then sauté in a mixture of oil and butter until golden brown.

Oven French Fries

When you can't give the cooking your full attention, it may be easier to bake chips to 'French-fried' crispness. The texture is a little different, but very good.

Metric/Imperial	*American*
500 g/1 lb old potatoes	1 lb old potatoes
1 teaspoon paprika	1 teaspoon paprika
50 g/2 oz butter, melted, or	¼ cup butter, melted, or
4 tablespoons oil	4 tablespoons oil
salt	salt

Peel the potatoes and cut into sticks about 1 cm/½ inch thick. Dry well with kitchen paper towels. Spread in a single layer in a shallow baking pan and sprinkle with paprika. Pour butter or oil over and turn until coated.

Place in a preheated very hot oven (230°C/450°F, Gas Mark 8) and bake for 30 to 40 minutes, turning several times, until golden brown and tender. Drain on crumpled paper towels. Serve sprinkled with a little salt. Serves 4.

Helpful Hints

Do not store potatoes near strong smelling foods or chemicals like methylated spirits and paraffin. The potatoes will absorb their odours.

ROAST POTATOES

Preparation Choose medium even-sized potatoes. Peel and parboil them in salted water for 5 to 10 minutes if desired. Drain well and pat dry.

To roast Heat lard or dripping from roast meat in a roasting pan, using sufficient to cover the bottom of the pan. Place the potatoes in the hot fat, baste and cook, uncovered, in a preheated hot oven (220°C/435°F, Gas Mark 7) for about 1 hour or until crisp and golden. Turn and baste occasionally with the hot fat. Alternatively, arrange parboiled potatoes around roast meat and cook for the last hour of cooking time.

To serve Drain off the fat and place in a warmed serving dish or arrange around roast meat on serving dish. Do not cover or the potatoes will lose their crispness. Serve as soon as possible.

Freezer note: If roast potatoes are to be frozen, prepare as above and cook in a preheated moderately hot oven (200°C/400°F, Gas Mark 6) for 45 minutes, basting occasionally. Drain off the fat and cool. Place the potatoes in freezer bags and seal. To serve from the freezer, unwrap and place frozen potatoes in a roasting pan with additional hot fat or oil. Reheat in a hot oven for 30 minutes.

Variation

Parmentier Potatoes Peel and cut old potatoes into 1 cm/ ½ inch cubes. Heat fat (a mixture of oil and margarine or butter gives a good flavour) in a roasting pan and add the potatoes. Toss gently until they are coated in fat. Bake in a preheated moderately hot oven (200°C/400°F, Gas Mark 6) for 30 to 40 minutes until the potatoes are golden brown. Drain, sprinkle with salt and pepper to taste and place in a warmed serving dish. Do not cover. Serve with meat, poultry or fish dishes.

Helpful Hints

Chips will be much crisper if soaked in ice cold water before cooking. Always dry thoroughly in kitchen paper or a tea towel before frying.

Do not buy potatoes that are damaged, misshapen, shrivelled or green and handle them carefully to prevent bruising.

Perfect Roast Potatoes

Crispy Roast Potatoes with Herbs

Metric/Imperial	*American*
750 g/1½ lb potatoes, peeled	1½ lb potatoes, peeled
50 g/2 oz dripping or lard	¼ cup drippings or lard
1 egg, beaten	1 egg, beaten
2 garlic cloves, crushed (optional)	2 garlic cloves, crushed (optional)
grated rind of 1 orange	grated rind of 1 orange
grated rind of 1 lemon	grated rind of 1 lemon
salt and pepper	salt and pepper
50 g/2 oz plain flour	½ cup all-purpose flour
50 g/2 oz sage and onion stuffing mix	½ cup sage and onion stuffing mix

Cut the potatoes into small, even-sized pieces. Boil for 5 minutes in salted water, then drain. Place the dripping or lard in a roasting pan and preheat in a moderately hot oven (200°C/400°F, Gas Mark 6).

Mix together the egg, garlic (if used), orange and lemon rind, salt and pepper. Coat the potato pieces with flour, then dip in the egg mixture and finally coat with the dry stuffing mix.

Place the potatoes in the hot fat and baste well. Roast for 1 hour at the above temperature, turning once. Drain on kitchen paper towels and transfer to a warmed serving dish. Serves 4.

POTATO DOUGHS

The potato is a far more versatile vegetable than most people realize. The addition of potato gives bread and pastry doughs and cakes a beautiful soft, moist consistency. Make extra mashed potato and reserve some to add to bread and pastry doughs or cakes (see page 90).

Basic Potato Bread

This basic dough can also be used to make savoury rolls, pizzas, croissants or any recipe requiring a bread dough.

Metric/Imperial	American
2 teaspoons dried yeast	2 teaspoons active dry yeast
½ teaspoon sugar	½ teaspoon sugar
300 ml/½ pint warm water	1¼ cups warm water
250 g/½ lb strong white flour	2 cups strong white flour
250 g/½ lb wholewheat flour	2 cups wholewheat flour
2 teaspoons salt	2 teaspoons salt
125 g/4 oz mashed potato, sieved	½ cup sieved mashed potato

Sprinkle the yeast and sugar on to the water. Stir and leave in a warm place for 10 minutes or until frothy.

Mix the flours and salt in a bowl and rub in the mashed potato. Add the yeast liquid and mix to a soft dough.

Turn on to a floured surface and knead for 10 minutes until smooth and elastic. Place the dough in an oiled polythene bag, or a clean bowl covered with oiled plastic wrap. Leave in a warm place for 1 hour or until the dough has doubled in size.

Knock back (punch down) the dough to its original volume and knead for 1 to 2 minutes. Shape the dough and place in a greased 1 kg/2 lb loaf tin. Cover and leave to prove in a warm place for about 45 minutes until doubled in size.

Brush the surface with milk and bake in a preheated hot oven (230°C/450°F, Gas Mark 8) for 45 to 50 minutes until the bread is well risen and sounds hollow when tapped underneath. Turn out of the tin and cool on a wire rack. Makes one 1 kg/2 lb loaf.

Variation

Bread Rolls After knocking back (punching down) and kneading the dough for 1 to 2 minutes, divide it into 16 pieces and shape into rolls. Arrange on greased baking sheets, cover and leave to prove in a warm place for about 25 minutes or until well risen.

Brush the rolls with milk or beaten egg. Place in a preheated hot oven (230°C/450°F, Gas Mark 8) and bake for 15 minutes or until golden. Cool on a wire rack.

Basic Potato Pastry (Dough)

This potato pastry is ideal for pastry bases and freezes well. This recipe makes sufficient to line a 20 cm/8 inch flan dish.

Metric/Imperial	*American*
175 g/6 oz plain flour	1½ cups all-purpose flour
½ teaspoon salt	½ teaspoon salt
40 g/1½ oz margarine	3 tablespoons margarine
40 g/1½ oz lard	3 tablespoons shortening
75 g/3 oz mashed potato, sieved	¾ cup sieved mashed potato

Sift the flour and salt into a bowl. Rub in the fats until the mixture resembles fine breadcrumbs. Work in the potato to make a firm dough.

Turn on to a lightly floured surface and knead until smooth. Use as required.

Variation

Wholewheat Potato Pastry (Dough) Use the recipe above but replace the plain flour with wholewheat flour and increase the fats to 50 g/2 oz (¼ cup) each.

Helpful Hint

The water in which potatoes have been cooked should not be thrown away. It contains valuable nutrients so use it in soups, stocks, sauces or gravy. Or use it when making bread, the potato water helps give a lighter loaf and improves its keeping qualities.

Family Meals

Parsley Potato Cakes, Rosemary and Garlic Sauté Potatoes, page 32

Parsley Potato Cakes

Metric/Imperial	American
350 g/12 oz potatoes, boiled and mashed	¾ lb potatoes, boiled and mashed
125 g/4 oz cream cheese (optional)	½ cup cream cheese (optional)
125 g/4 oz plain flour	1 cup all-purpose flour
salt and pepper	salt and pepper
50 g/2 oz butter	¼ cup butter
2 tablespoons chopped parsley	2 tablespoons chopped parsley

Place hot mashed potato in a large bowl and gradually work in the cheese, if using, flour and salt and pepper to taste. Cut the butter into tiny pieces and stir into the potato mixture. Stir in the parsley and continue to beat until smooth.

Turn out on to a floured surface and roll out very lightly, using plenty of flour, until about 5 mm/¼ inch thick. Heat a griddle or heavy-based frying pan and grease lightly. Using a floured 75 cm/3 inch pastry cutter cut the potato mixture into rounds and cook on the griddle or pan until golden brown on both sides. Serve with bacon and eggs, or cooked ham. Makes about 20.

Chicken Marengo

Metric/Imperial	American
2 tablespoons oil	2 tablespoons oil
4 chicken pieces, skinned	1 broiler, cut into 4 and skinned
500 g/1 lb small new potatoes, scrubbed	1 lb small new potatoes, scrubbed
1 onion, chopped	1 onion, chopped
2 carrots, sliced	2 carrots, sliced
250 g/8 oz tomatoes, skinned and chopped	1 cup peeled and chopped tomatoes
125 g/4 oz mushrooms, sliced	1 cup sliced mushrooms
2 tablespoons tomato purée	2 tablespoons tomato paste
50 g/2 oz cornflour	⅓ cup cornstarch
600 ml/1 pint chicken stock	2½ cups chicken stock
4 tablespoons sherry	4 tablespoons sherry
salt and pepper	salt and pepper
chopped parsley, to garnish	chopped parsley, for garnish

Heat the oil in a large saucepan and cook the chicken until brown all over. Remove with a slotted spoon and place in a casserole with the potatoes. Add the onion and carrots to the pan and sauté for 5 minutes, then add the tomatoes and mushrooms and cook for a further 2 minutes. Blend together the tomato purée (paste) and cornflour (cornstarch) and add to the vegetables. Blend in the stock and bring to the boil, stirring, then add the sherry and salt and pepper to taste.

Pour over the chicken and potatoes, cover and cook in a preheated moderate oven (180°C/350°F, Gas Mark 4) for 1 hour or until the chicken and potatoes are tender. Add a little more stock or water if the casserole is becoming too dry. Serve garnished with parsley. Serves 4.

Fish Chowder

Metric/Imperial	American
50 g/2 oz butter	¼ cup butter
1 onion, sliced	1 onion, sliced
125 g/4 oz bacon, rinds removed and chopped	6 bacon slices, rinds removed and chopped
4 celery sticks, chopped	4 stalks celery, chopped
1 small green pepper, cored, seeded and diced	1 small green pepper, seeded and diced
175 g/6 oz potato, peeled and diced	1 cup peeled and diced potato
300 ml/½ pint fish or chicken stock	1¼ cups fish or chicken stock
750 g/1½ lb smoked and white fish, skinned and cubed	1½ lb smoked and white fish, skinned and cubed
300 ml/½ pint milk	1¼ cups milk
1 tablespoon cornflour	1 tablespoon cornstarch
salt and pepper	salt and pepper
parsley, to garnish	parsley, for garnish

Melt the butter in a large saucepan and sauté the onion, bacon, celery, pepper and potato for 5 minutes. Add the stock and simmer for 20 minutes or until the potatoes are tender. Stir in the fish and cook for 5 minutes.

Blend together the milk and cornflour (cornstarch) and add to the chowder. Return to the boil and add salt and pepper to taste. Simmer for 5 minutes, then pour into a warmed soup tureen and garnish with parsley. Serves 6.

Minted Potato Chops

Metric/Imperial	American
500 g/1 lb potatoes, peeled and sliced	1 lb potatoes, peeled and sliced
salt and pepper	salt and pepper
4 lamb leg bone steaks	4 lamb leg bone steaks
25 g/1 oz butter, melted	2 tablespoons melted butter
1 tablespoon freshly chopped mint	1 tablespoon freshly chopped mint

Place the potato slices in the bottom of a greased ovenproof dish. Sprinkle with salt and pepper, then place the lamb on top and sprinkle with more salt and pepper.

Mix together the butter and mint and spoon over the meat and potatoes. Cover the dish and cook in a preheated moderate oven (180°C/350°F, Gas Mark 4) for 30 minutes. Uncover the dish, increase the oven temperature to hot (220°C/425°F, Gas Mark 7) and cook for a further 15 minutes or until meat and potatoes are tender. Serve hot with baked tomatoes and a green salad. Serves 4.

Creamy Fish Savoury

Metric/Imperial	American
4 × 175 g/6 oz sole fillets	4 × 6 oz sole fillets
50 g/2 oz plain flour	½ cup all-purpose flour
salt and pepper	salt and pepper
50 g/2 oz butter	¼ cup butter
1 bunch spring onions, chopped	1 bunch scallions, chopped
150 ml/¼ pint milk	⅔ cup milk
150 ml/¼ pint single cream	⅔ cup light cream
125 g/4 oz peeled prawns	⅔ cup shelled shrimp
500 g/1 lb potatoes, boiled, mashed and sieved (see page 22)	1 lb potatoes, boiled, mashed and sieved (see page 22)
parsley, to garnish	parsley, for garnish

Skin the sole fillets and toss in the flour, salt and pepper. Melt the butter in a frying pan and cook the fish for 4 minutes or until it becomes opaque, turning once. Add the onions (scallions), milk, cream and salt and pepper to taste. Do not stir, just shake the pan a little and cook for 5 minutes. Stir in the prawns (shrimp) and heat through. Transfer to a hot serving dish and pipe the hot mashed potato around the edge. Sprinkle with parsley. Serves 4.

Helpful Hint
If the potatoes are to be prepared in advance of cooking leave them soaking in cold water to cover. This prevents discoloration (although it does result in a slight loss of the water soluble vitamins).

Beef Moussaka

Metric/Imperial	American
1 tablespoon oil	1 tablespoon oil
1 onion, chopped	1 onion, chopped
500 g/1 lb lean minced beef	2 cups firmly packed ground beef
1 garlic clove, crushed	1 garlic clove, crushed
salt and pepper	salt and pepper
1 teaspoon dried oregano	1 teaspoon dried oregano
1 tablespoon chopped parsley	1 tablespoon chopped parsley
1 × 450 g/15 oz can tomatoes	1 × 16 oz can tomatoes
1 aubergine, sliced and parboiled	1 eggplant, sliced and parboiled
500 g/1 lb potatoes, parboiled	1 lb potatoes, parboiled
Topping:	Topping:
2 eggs	2 eggs
5 tablespoons soured cream	5 tablespoons sour cream
5 tablespoons milk	5 tablespoons milk
75 g/3 oz Cheddar cheese, grated	¾ cup grated Cheddar cheese,

Heat the oil in a pan and sauté the onion for 5 minutes. Add the beef and cook, stirring, for 5 minutes. Stir in the garlic powder, salt and pepper, oregano, parsley and tomatoes with their juice. Bring to the boil, cover and simmer for 30 minutes. Transfer the meat to an ovenproof dish and arrange the aubergine (eggplant) slices on top. Slice the potatoes thinly and arrange overlapping over the top.

To make the topping, beat together the eggs, soured cream and milk and pour over the potatoes. Sprinkle with the cheese and bake in a preheated moderately hot oven (190°C/375°F, Gas Mark 5) for 30 minutes or until bubbling and golden. Serve hot with a green or mixed salad. Serves 4-6.

Variation

If preferred, the meat mixture can be layered with the aubergine (eggplant) and potatoes.

Farmers' Sausage Pie

Metric/Imperial	American
500 g/1 lb sausage meat	1 lb sausage meat
½ teaspoon dried mixed herbs	½ teaspoon dried mixed herbs
50 g/2 oz streaky bacon, rinds removed and chopped	3 fatty bacon slices, rinds removed and chopped
2 tomatoes, sliced	2 tomatoes, sliced
salt and pepper	salt and pepper
1 cooking apple, peeled, cored and sliced	1 tart apple, peeled, cored and sliced
125 g/4 oz Cheddar cheese, grated	1 cup grated Cheddar cheese
1 kg/2 lb potatoes, boiled and mashed (see page 22)	2 lb potatoes, boiled and mashed (see page 22)

Place the sausage meat in the bottom of a 1.75 litre/3 pint (7½ cup) ovenproof dish. Sprinkle with the mixed herbs. Place the bacon in a frying pan and cook gently in its own fat. Drain, then place over the sausage meat with the tomato slices, salt and pepper and apple. Mix the cheese with the mashed potato and spread over the dish. Bake in a preheated moderate oven (180°C/350°F, Gas Mark 4) for 1 hour or until cooked through and golden. Serve hot with a green salad. Serves 4.

Farmers' Sausage Pie

Piquant Fish Pie

Metric/Imperial	*American*
25 g/1 oz butter	2 tablespoons butter
25 g/1 oz plain flour	¼ cup all-purpose flour
300 ml/½ pint milk	1¼ cups milk
2 tablespoons salad cream	2 tablespoons salad cream
4 large gherkins, sliced	4 large gherkins, sliced
1 teaspoon lemon juice	1 teaspoon lemon juice
salt and pepper	salt and pepper
500 g/1 lb white fish	1 lb white fish
2 large tomatoes, sliced	2 large tomatoes, sliced
750 g/1½ lb potatoes, boiled, mashed and sieved (see page 22)	1½ lb potatoes, boiled, mashed and sieved (see page 22)
50 g/2 oz Cheddar cheese, grated	½ cup grated Cheddar cheese

Melt the butter in a pan, then stir in the flour and cook for 1 minute. Remove from the heat and gradually stir in the milk. Cook, stirring continuously, until the sauce thickens. Continue to cook for 1 minute. Stir in the salad cream, gherkins, lemon juice, salt and pepper. Divide the fish into 4 and place in a shallow 1.2 litre/2 pint ovenproof dish. Pour the sauce over and cover with the tomato slices.

Place the potato in a piping (pastry) bag fitted with a large star nozzle and pipe rosettes over the top. Sprinkle with the cheese and bake in a preheated moderately hot oven (190°C/375°F, Gas Mark 5) for 30 minutes or until golden. Serve hot. Serves 4.

Irish Stew

Metric/Imperial	*American*
1 kg/2 lb potatoes, sliced	2 lb potatoes, sliced
250 g/8 oz onions, sliced	2 cups sliced onion
1.25 kg/2½ lb middle neck of lamb chops, trimmed	2½ lb neck lamb chops, trimmed
450 ml/¾ pint chicken stock	2 cups chicken stock
salt and pepper	salt and pepper
parsley to garnish	parsley for garnish

Place the potatoes and onions in a large saucepan and arrange the lamb chops on top. Pour over the stock and add generous amounts of salt and pepper. Bring to the boil, cover and simmer for 1½ hours or until the meat is tender. Transfer to a warmed serving dish and sprinkle with parsley. Serves 4.

Cabbage Hotpot

Metric/Imperial	American
2 large chicken pieces	½ broiler
2 tablespoons oil	2 tablespoons oil
250 g/8 oz onions, sliced	2 cups chopped onion
500 g/1 lb Dutch cabbage, shredded	1 lb Dutch cabbage, shredded
2 tablespoons plain flour	2 tablespoons all-purpose flour
2 tablespoons vinegar	2 tablespoons vinegar
300 ml/½ pint chicken stock	1¼ cups chicken stock
2 tablespoons demerara sugar	2 tablespoons brown sugar
salt and pepper	salt and pepper
500 g/1 lb potatoes, peeled and sliced	1 lb potatoes, peeled and sliced
25 g/1 oz butter, melted	2 tablespoons melted butter

Remove all the meat from the chicken bones and cut into small pieces. (Use the bones to make the stock.) Heat the oil in a frying pan (skillet), add the chicken meat and sauté quickly until beginning to brown. Remove the chicken from the pan using a slotted spoon.

Add the onions to the pan and fry in the remaining oil for 5 minutes until beginning to soften but not brown. Stir in the cabbage and cook until all the oil is absorbed.

Mix in the flour, vinegar, stock, sugar, salt and pepper. Bring to the boil, then stir in the chicken meat. Transfer to a 1.75 litre/3 pint (7½ cup) ovenproof dish and cover with the sliced potatoes. Brush with the melted butter and cook in a preheated moderate oven (180°C/350°F, Gas Mark 4) for about 1½ hours until the potatoes are cooked and golden. Serve immediately with a selection of homemade pickles. Serves 4.

Mackerel Lattice Pie

Mackerel Lattice Pie

Metric/Imperial
25 g/1 oz butter
1 tablespoon oil
250 g/8 oz courgettes,
 sliced
125 g/4 oz mushrooms,
 sliced
1 × 450 g/15 oz can
 tomatoes
salt and pepper
½ teaspoon ground ginger
 (optional)
2 mackerel, each cut into
 2 fillets
750 g/1½ lb potatoes,
 boiled, mashed and
 sieved (see page 22)
125 g/4 oz red Leicester
 cheese, grated

American
2 tablespoons butter
1 tablespoon oil
2 cups sliced
 zucchini
1 cup sliced
 mushrooms
1 × 16 oz can
 tomatoes
salt and pepper
½ teaspoon ground ginger
 (optional)
2 mackerel, each cut into
 2 fillets
1½ lb potatoes, boiled,
 mashed and sieved
 (see page 22)
1 cup grated red Leicester
 cheese

Heat the butter and oil in a pan and sauté the courgettes
(zucchini) and mushrooms until just soft. Stir in the
tomatoes and their juice, bring to the boil and season with

salt, pepper and ginger, if used. Place half the mixture in the bottom of an ovenproof dish, cover with 2 mackerel fillets, then repeat the layers.

Mix together the potato and cheese, then place in a piping (pastry) bag fitted with a large star nozzle. Pipe diagonal lines of potato across the dish, then across the other way. Cook in a preheated moderately hot oven (190°C/375°F, Gas Mark 5) for 30 minutes or until the potato is golden. Serve hot. Serves 4-6.

Fish Cakes

Metric/Imperial	American
250 g/8 oz cod	½ lb cod
milk	milk
salt and pepper	salt and pepper
500 g/1 lb potatoes, boiled and mashed (see page 22)	1 lb potatoes, boiled and mashed (see page 22)
1 tablespoon chopped parsley	1 tablespoon chopped parsley
2 eggs, beaten	2 eggs, beaten
flour	flour
dry breadcrumbs	dry bread crumbs
oil, for frying	oil, for frying
parsley, to garnish	parsley, for garnish

Place the cod in a pan and just cover with milk. Sprinkle with salt and pepper, cover and bring slowly to the boil. Remove from the heat and leave the fish, covered, for 5 minutes. Drain off the liquid, and reserve for a sauce or soup, if liked. Skin the fish, flake roughly and remove any bones.

Mix the fish with the mashed potato and parsley. Add salt and pepper to taste and a little of the beaten egg to bind. Turn the mixture on to a floured surface and form into a roll. Cut into 8 slices and shape each into a cake. Coat the cakes with beaten egg and breadcrumbs. Heat oil for shallow or deep frying and cook the cakes until crisp and golden. Drain well, place on a warmed serving dish and garnish with parsley. Serve with a parsley or tomato sauce and a green vegetable. Serves 4.

Crusted Mince Roll

Metric/Imperial	*American*
350 g/12 oz potatoes, boiled and mashed (see page 22)	¾ lb potatoes, boiled and mashed (see page 22)
250 g/8 oz plain flour	2 cups all-purpose flour
3 teaspoons baking powder	3 teaspoons baking powder
1 teaspoon curry powder	1 teaspoon curry powder
½ teaspoon salt	½ teaspoon salt
125 g/4 oz shredded beef suet	¾ cup shredded beef suet
milk, to brush	milk, for brushing
Filling:	*Filling:*
250 g/8 oz lean minced beef	1 cup firmly packed ground beef
125 g/4 oz sausage meat	½ cup sausage meat
1 large onion, chopped	1 large onion, chopped
1 garlic clove, crushed	1 garlic clove, crushed
125 g/4 oz mushrooms, sliced	1 cup sliced mushrooms
1 green pepper, cored, seeded and chopped	1 green pepper, seeded and chopped
125 g/4 oz frozen mixed vegetables	¾ cup frozen mixed vegetables
1 tablespoon tomato purée	1 tablespoon tomato paste
1 teaspoon ground ginger	1 teaspoon ground ginger
150 ml/¼ pint beef stock	⅔ cup beef stock
salt and pepper	salt and pepper

Reserve 3 tablespoons mashed potato. Sift the flour, baking powder, curry powder and salt into a bowl. Add the suet and mashed potato, then mix together to make a dough. Wrap in plastic wrap and chill in the refrigerator until firm.

Meanwhile, to make the filling, place the beef in a pan with the sausage meat. Cook, stirring, until the meats are browned. Add the onion and garlic and continue cooking for 5 minutes. Stir in the mushrooms, pepper, mixed vegetables, tomato purée (paste), ginger, stock, salt and pepper. Continue cooking for 10 minutes, then stir in the reserved potato. Remove from the heat and allow to cool.

Roll out the pastry dough to 25×30 cm (10×12 inches). Spread the filling down the centre, leaving a narrow border. Dampen the edges and roll up from a short side. Brush with milk, then place the roll, join side down, on a greased piece of foil. Wrap the foil over the roll and place on a baking sheet. Cook in a preheated moderately hot oven (200°C/400°F, Gas Mark 6) for 30 to 40 minutes. The roll should be browned and may have split a little. Serve with hot vegetables. Serves 6-8.

Liver and Onion Savoury

Metric/Imperial	American
2 tablespoons plain flour	2 tablespoons all-purpose flour
salt and pepper	salt and pepper
750 g/1½ lb lamb's liver, thinly sliced	1½ lb lamb's liver, thinly sliced
2 tablespoons oil	2 tablespoons oil
2 onions, sliced	2 onions, sliced
150 ml/¼ pint stock	⅔ cup stock
150 ml/¼ pint apple juice	⅔ cup apple juice
700 g/1½ lb potatoes, parboiled	1½ lb potatoes, parboiled
25 g/1 oz butter	2 tablespoons butter
parsley, to garnish	parsley, for garnish

Season the flour with salt and pepper and toss the liver slices in it. Heat the oil in a frying pan (skillet) and sauté the onions for 3 minutes. Add the liver and cook until lightly browned on both sides. Stir in the stock and apple juice. Check the seasoning.

Arrange the liver mixture in an ovenproof dish. Slice the potatoes and place on top. Dot with the butter and cook in a preheated moderate oven (180°C/350°F, Gas Mark 4) for 25 to 30 minutes until the liver is tender. Serve hot, garnished with chopped parsley. Serves 4.

Variations

Liver Apple Savoury Add 2 peeled and sliced apples to the liver mixture.

Chicken and Onion Savoury Use 750 g/1½ lb chicken portions in place of liver.

Potato Braid

Potato Braid

Metric/Imperial
1 quantity Potato Pastry
  (see page 37)
Filling:
500 g/1 lb pork
  sausagemeat
salt and pepper
4 tablespoons chutney or
  pickle
250 g/8 oz cooked
  potatoes, sliced
50 g/2 oz Cheddar cheese,
  grated
1 egg, beaten, to glaze

American
1 quantity Potato Pastry
  (see page 37)
Filling:
1 lb pork sausage meat
salt and pepper
4 tablespoons
  relish
½ lb cooked potatoes,
  sliced
½ cup grated Cheddar
  cheese
1 egg, beaten, to glaze

Roll out the pastry to 30 cm × 25 cm (12 × 10 ins). Place on a baking sheet and mark into three pieces lengthwise.

Season the sausage meat with the salt and pepper and spread down the centre section. Cover the sausage meat with the pickle or chutney then lay the potato slices and cheese on top.

Make diagonal cuts 2.5 cm (1 inch) apart on each side of pastry to within 1 cm (½ inch) of the filling. Brush the strips with water and plait them over the filling. Press to seal and trim the ends. Brush with the beaten egg and bake in a preheated hot oven (220°C/425°F, Gas Mark 7) for 15 minutes, then reduce the temperature to moderately hot (200°C/400°F, Gas Mark 6) and bake for a further 25 to 30 minutes. Serve hot or cold. Serves 4-6.

Ham and Potato Bake

Metric/Imperial	American
50 g/2 oz margarine	¼ cup margarine
50 g/2 oz plain flour	½ cup all-purpose flour
600 ml/1 pint milk	2½ cups milk
salt and pepper	salt and pepper
½ teaspoon dried basil	½ teaspoon dried basil
½ teaspoon dried marjoram	½ teaspoon dried marjoram
750 g/1½ lb potatoes, sliced	1½ lb potatoes, sliced
500 g/1 lb onions, sliced	1 lb onions, sliced
250 g/8 oz cooked ham, sliced	½ lb cooked ham, sliced

Melt the margarine in a pan, then stir in the flour and cook for 1 minute. Remove from the heat and gradually stir in the milk. Cook, stirring, until the sauce thickens. Add salt and pepper, basil and marjoram.

In a greased ovenproof dish, layer the potatoes, onions and ham, sprinkling each layer with salt and pepper. Pour over the sauce. Cover and cook in a preheated moderate oven (180°C/350°F, Gas Mark 4) for 1 hour. Remove the lid and cook for a further 30 minutes until the vegetables are tender and the top browned. Serve hot with a green vegetable or tossed salad and garlic bread. Serves 4.

Curried Fish Parcels

Metric/Imperial	American
325 g/11 oz self-raising flour	2¾ cups self-rising flour
150 g/5 oz mashed and sieved potato (see page 22)	⅔ cups mashed and sieved potato (see page 22)
½ teaspoon salt	½ teaspoon salt
250 g/8 oz butter	1 cup butter
Filling:	*Filling:*
500 g/1 lb white fish	1 lb white fish
450 ml/¾ pint milk	2 cups milk
40 g/1½ oz butter	3 tablespoons butter
1 small onion, finely chopped	1 small onion, grated
40 g/1½ oz plain flour	6 tablespoons all-purpose flour
2 teaspoons curry paste	2 teaspoons curry paste
salt and pepper	salt and pepper
50 g/2 oz salted peanuts, chopped	½ cup chopped salted peanuts
50 g/2 oz sultanas	⅓ cup golden raisins
beaten egg, to glaze	beaten egg, for glazing

To make the pastry, mix together the flour, potatoes, salt and a little water to make a firm dough. Knead until smooth, then chill in the refrigerator for 10 minutes.

On a floured surface, roll out the pastry to a narrow rectangle approximately 45×13 cm (18×5 inches). Dot the butter over two-thirds of the strip. Fold into three, turn, roll out and repeat folding and rolling. Fold again and chill in the refrigerator for 30 minutes. Roll out, fold and turn three more times, then wrap in plastic wrap and chill in the refrigerator for 2 hours.

Meanwhile, prepare the filling. Poach the fish in the milk for 10 minutes or until tender, then drain, reserving the milk. Flake the fish, removing any skin or bones. Melt the butter in a pan and sauté the onion for 5 minutes. Stir in the flour and cook for 1 minute. Remove from the heat and gradually stir in the reserved milk. Cook, stirring, until the sauce thickens. Stir in the curry paste, salt and pepper and continue to cook for 1 minute (the sauce should be of a binding consistency). Add the fish to the sauce with the peanuts and sultanas (golden raisins), allow to cool.

Roll out the pastry (dough) on a floured surface and divide into 6 equal squares, reserving the trimmings. Divide the filling between the squares. Moisten the edges of the pastry (dough) with water, fold diagonally over the filling to form triangles and knock up the edges with the back of a knife to seal.

Make a hole in the top of each parcel and decorate with the pastry (dough) trimmings. Place on a wet baking sheet and brush with beaten egg.

Cook in a preheated moderately hot oven (200°C/400°F, Gas Mark 6) for 30 minutes or until the pastry (dough) is well risen and golden. Serve hot with a green vegetable or salad. Serves 6.

Savoury Kebabs

Metric/Imperial	American
250 g/8 oz piece cooked ham	½ lb piece cooked ham
500 g/1 lb new potatoes, parboiled	1 lb new potatoes, parboiled
8 tomatoes, halved	8 tomatoes, halved
8 bay leaves	8 bay leaves
12 button mushrooms	12 button mushrooms
oil, to brush	oil, for brushing
boiled rice, to serve	boiled rice, to serve

Cut the ham into 2.5 cm (1 inch) cubes. Cut any large potatoes so the pieces are of similar size.

Thread the ingredients on to 4 skewers and brush with oil. Cook under a preheated grill or on a barbecue for 7 to 10 minutes, turning frequently. Serve on a bed of boiled rice with a salad. Serves 4.

Helpful Hint
It is best to buy new potatoes in small quantities and use them up quickly so that you can appreciate their fresh flavour. To test freshness, check that the skins rub off easily and that the potatoes are damp to touch.

Breakfast and Brunch Dishes

Irish Potato Cakes

Metric/Imperial	American
500 g/1 lb potatoes, boiled and mashed (see page 22)	1 lb potatoes, boiled and mashed (see page 22)
50 g/2 oz butter	¼ cup butter
salt and pepper	salt and pepper
125 g/4 oz plain flour	1 cup all-purpose flour
butter, to serve	butter, to serve

Beat together the potato, butter, salt and pepper. Work in enough flour to bind to a dough.

Divide the dough into 2 and pat or roll each piece into a round about 1 cm/½ inch thick. Cut each round into 6 or 8 triangles.

Heat a griddle or heavy-based frying pan (skillet) and grease thoroughly. Lift the potato cakes carefully on to the griddle with a spatula and cook for about 5 minutes on each side. Keep warm in a folded tea towel. To serve, split in half and spread with butter. Serve with sausages, bacon, tomatoes or eggs. As a sweet dish, serve with golden syrup. Makes 12-16.

Potato Oatcakes

Metric/Imperial	American
500 g/1 lb potatoes, boiled, mashed and sieved (see page 22)	1 lb potatoes, boiled, mashed and sieved (see page 22)
175 g/6 oz fine oatmeal	1 cup fine oatmeal
1 teaspoon salt	1 teaspoon salt
milk, to bind	milk, for binding

Mix together the potato, oatmeal and salt. Add enough milk to form a stiff dough.

Turn on to a floured surface and knead until smooth. Roll out thinly, prick all over with a fork and cut out rounds with a 7.5 cm/3 inch pastry cutter.

Heat a griddle or heavy-based frying pan (skillet) and grease thoroughly. Cook the oatcakes for 2 minutes each side. Serve hot or cold with butter. Makes 12-15 oatcakes.

Pytt I Parna

Metric/Imperial
25 g/1 oz butter
3 tablespoons oil
750 g/1½ lb potatoes,
   peeled and diced
2 onions, chopped
350 g/12 oz cooked meat,
   diced
salt and pepper
1 tablespoon chopped
   parsley
4 eggs

American
2 tablespoons butter
3 tablespoons oil
1½ lb potatoes, peeled and
   diced
2 onions, chopped
1½ cups diced cooked
   meat
salt and pepper
1 tablespoon chopped
   parsley
4 eggs

Melt the butter in a pan and add 1 tablespoon oil. Sauté the potatoes, stirring and turning, for about 20 minutes until cooked and evenly browned. Remove from the pan.

Heat 1 tablespoon oil in the pan and add the onion and meat. Cook, stirring, until evenly browned, then return the potatoes to the pan. Add salt and pepper and the parsley, then heat through.

Heat the remaining oil in a frying pan and fry the eggs. Spoon the potato mixture on to 4 warmed serving plates and top each with a freshly fried egg. Serve immediately. Serves 4.

Pytt I Parna

Egg Potato Rings

Metric/Imperial	*American*
500 g/1 lb potatoes, boiled and mashed (see page 22)	1 lb potatoes, boiled and mashed (see page 22)
50 g/2 oz butter	¼ cup butter
salt and pepper	salt and pepper
4 eggs	4 eggs
2 tomatoes, skinned and chopped	2 tomatoes, peeled and chopped
1 tablespoon milk	1 tablespoon milk
parsley, to garnish	parsley, for garnish

Beat the potato with 15 g/½ oz (1 tablespoon) butter and salt and pepper to taste. Divide into 4 and shape each piece into a round about 1 cm/½ inch thick. Remove the centres with a small pastry cutter.

Heat 25 g/1 oz (2 tablespoons) butter in a frying pan (skillet) and cook the rings and centres until golden brown on both sides. Drain and keep warm on a serving plate.

Beat together the eggs, tomatoes, milk and salt and pepper to taste. Heat the remaining butter in a saucepan and lightly scramble the eggs. Spoon into the potato rings and top with the centres. Serve immediately, garnish with parsley. Serves 4.

Corn Tatties

Metric/Imperial	*American*
1 tablespoon oil	1 tablespoon oil
1 onion, chopped	1 onion, chopped
250 g/8 oz streaky bacon, rinds removed and chopped	12 fatty bacon slices, rinds removed and chopped
1 × 200 g/7 oz can sweetcorn, drained	1 × 7 oz can corn kernels, drained
500 g/1 lb potatoes, boiled and sliced	1 lb potatoes, boiled and sliced
3 eggs	3 eggs
salt and pepper	salt and pepper
chopped parsley	chopped parsley

Heat the oil in a pan and sauté the onion for 5 minutes. Add the bacon and cook for a further 5 minutes, then stir in the corn.

Arrange the potatoes in the bottom of a greased oven-proof dish. Cover with the corn and bacon mixture. Beat the eggs with plenty of salt and pepper and pour over the top. Sprinkle with a little parsley. Cook in a preheated moderately hot oven (190°C/375°F, Gas Mark 5) for 30 minutes or until set and lightly browned on top. Serve hot with toast or rolls. Serves 4.

Potato Omelette

Metric/Imperial	American
500 g/1 lb potatoes, boiled and mashed (see page 22)	1 lb potatoes, boiled and mashed (see page 22)
3 eggs, separated	3 eggs, separated
125 g/4 oz Cheddar cheese, grated	1 cup grated Cheddar cheese
2 tablespoons milk	2 tablespoons milk
1 tablespoon chopped parsley	1 tablespoon chopped parsley
salt and pepper	salt and pepper
25 g/1 oz butter	2 tablespons butter
To garnish:	*For garnish:*
cucumber slices	cucumber slices
tomato slices	tomato slices
chopped parsley	chopped parsley

Beat together the potato, egg yolks, cheese, milk, parsley, salt and pepper. Whisk the egg whites until stiff and fold into the potato mixture.

Melt the butter in a frying pan (skillet), pour in the mixture and cook for 2 minutes until the underside is set and lightly browned. Turn carefully and cook the other side for 2 minutes.

Slide on to a warmed serving plate and cut into quarters. Garnish each portion with cucumber, tomato and parsley. Serve with grilled tomatoes and toast. Serves 4.

Variation

Add diced cooked meat to the mixture.

Potato Galette

Metric/Imperial	American
750 g/1½ lb potatoes, boiled and mashed (see page 22)	1½ lb potatoes, boiled and mashed (see page 22)
50 g/2 oz butter	¼ cup butter
2 tablespoons milk	2 tablespoons milk
175 g/6 oz Cheddar cheese, grated	1½ cups grated Cheddar cheese
250 g/8 oz onions, finely chopped	1½ cups grated onion
1 egg, beaten	1 egg, beaten
salt and pepper	salt and pepper
2 tomatoes, sliced	2 tomatoes, sliced
125 g/4 oz streaky bacon, chopped	6 fatty bacon slices, chopped

Mix the potato with the butter and milk. Beat in 125 g/4 oz (1 cup) cheese, the onion, egg, salt and pepper. Turn on to a 23 cm/9 inch ovenproof plate and mould to form a base.

Arrange the tomato slices on top and sprinkle with the bacon and remaining cheese. Place in a preheated moderately hot oven (200°C/400°F, Gas Mark 6) for 20 to 30 minutes until the base is firm and the cheese melted. Serve hot. Serves 4.

Swiss Mushroom Savoury

Metric/Imperial	American
1 kg/2 lb potatoes, parboiled	2 lb potatoes, parboiled
350 g/12 oz button mushrooms	3 cups button mushrooms
2 tablespoons oil	2 tablespoons oil
1 onion, finely chopped	1 onion, grated
salt and pepper	salt and pepper
8 streaky bacon rashers, rinds removed	8 fatty bacon slices, rinds removed
8 pork chipolata sausages	8 small pork sausage links
1 tomato, cut in wedges	1 tomato, cut in wedges
parsley sprigs	parsley sprigs

Swiss Mushroom Savoury

Coarsely grate the potatoes. Finely chop 125 g/4 oz (1 cup) of the mushrooms. Heat 1 tablespoon oil in a frying pan and sauté the mushrooms and onion for 5 minutes. Add to the potato with plenty of seasoning, mix well.

Heat the remaining oil in the frying pan and add the potato mixture. Press into a large cake and fry until the underside is brown. Turn carefully with the help of a plate and brown the other side. Keep warm over a low heat.

Stretch the bacon rashers (slices), roll up and thread on to a skewer. Place the sausages and bacon under a pre-heated moderate grill (broiler) and cook for 10 to 15 minutes, turning frequently, until golden brown. Arrange the sausages, radiating from the centre, on top of the potato cake with the bacon rolls in between.

Remove the grill (broiler) grid, toss the remaining mushrooms in the fat, then grill (broil) for 2 to 3 minutes. Transfer the potato cake to a warmed serving dish and arrange the mushrooms around the edge of the cake. Garnish with tomato and parsley and serve hot. Serves 4.

Smoked Haddock Nests

Metric/Imperial	American
500 g/1 lb potatoes, boiled and mashed (see page 22)	1 lb potatoes, boiled and mashed (see page 22)
1 tablespoon cream	1 tablespoon cream
grated nutmeg	grated nutmeg
350 g/12 oz smoked haddock, cooked, skinned and flaked	¾ lb smoked haddock, cooked, skinned and flaked
salt and pepper	salt and pepper
4 eggs	4 eggs
75 g/3 oz Cheddar cheese, grated	¾ cup grated Cheddar cheese

Beat together the potatoes, cream, nutmeg, haddock and salt and pepper to taste. Place the mixture in the bottom of a greased shallow ovenproof dish.

Make 4 hollows in the mixture and break an egg into each. Sprinkle the cheese over the top and cook in a preheated moderate over (180°C/350°F, Gas Mark 4) for 30 minutes or until the eggs are just set. Serve immediately. Serves 4.

Variation

Make individual nests using 4 ovenproof ramekin dishes.

Corned Beef Floddies

Metric/Imperial	American
250 g/8 oz potatoes, peeled and grated	½ lb potatoes, peeled and grated
2 onions, peeled and grated	2 onions, peeled and grated
1 × 200 g/7 oz can corned beef, mashed	1 × 7 oz can corned beef, mashed
2 eggs	2 eggs
50 g/2 oz self-raising flour	½ cup self-rising flour
salt and pepper	salt and pepper
½ teaspoon made mustard	½ teaspoon prepared mustard
oil, for frying	oil, for frying

Mix together the potato, onion and corned beef. Beat the eggs and gradually blend in the flour. Add salt and pepper and the mustard and beat until smooth, then add to the potato mixture and mix well.

Heat a little oil in a frying pan (skillet) and drop spoonfuls of the mixture into the hot oil. Fry on both sides until crisp and brown. Drain and serve hot with toast. Serves 4.

Bubble and Squeak Pizza

Metric/Imperial	American
500 g/1 lb potatoes, boiled and mashed (see page 22)	1 lb potatoes, boiled and mashed (see page 22)
250 g/8 oz cabbage, cooked and chopped	½ lb cabbage, cooked and chopped
salt and pepper	salt and pepper
50 g/2 oz unsalted butter	¼ cup unsalted butter
Topping:	Topping:
1 tablespoon oil	1 tablespoon oil
1 small onion, chopped	1 small onion, chopped
1 × 225 g/8 oz can baked beans	1 × 8 oz can baked beans
1 × 175 g/6 oz canned ham, diced	1 × 175 g/6 oz canned ham, diced
1 teaspoon Worcestershire sauce	1 teaspoon Worcestershire sauce
parsley, to garnish	parsley, for garnish

Mix the potato and cabbage together and add salt and pepper to taste. Melt the butter in a frying pan (skillet) and add the mixture. Press into a cake and cook slowly until the underside is brown. Turn carefully with the help of a plate and cook the other side until brown. Transfer to a warmed serving plate and keep hot.

To make the topping, heat the oil in a pan and sauté the onion for 5 minutes. Stir in the beans, bacon grill and Worcestershire sauce. Heat gently and spoon on to the potato base. Serve hot, garnished with parsley. Serves 4.
Variation
Any leftover green vegetable can be used in place of the cooked cabbage.

Wholefood Dishes

Wholewheat Vegetable Pasties

Metric/Imperial	American
1 quantity Wholewheat Potato Pastry (see page 37)	1 quantity Wholewheat Potato Pastry (see page 37)
Filling:	*Filling:*
125 g/4 oz broad beans	1 cup lima beans
250 g/8 oz turnip, diced	2 cups diced turnip
250 g/8 oz carrot, grated	2 cups grated carrot
2 tablespoons chopped fresh chives	2 tablespoons chopped fresh chives
4 tablespoons mayonnaise	4 tablespoons mayonnaise
salt and pepper	salt and pepper
beaten egg, to glaze	beaten egg, to glaze

Filling Cook the beans and turnips in boiling, salted water for 10 minutes or until just tender. Drain well, then stir in the carrot, chives, mayonnaise and salt and pepper. Leave on one side to cool.

On a floured surface, roll out the potato dough to 3 mm/⅛ inch thickness and cut out 4 × 16.5 mm/6½ inch circles, using a saucer as a guide. Divide the filling between the pastry rounds. Moisten the edges then lift them up over the filling to enclose it completely and form the shape of a Cornish pasty. Seal the edges and scallop them. Brush all over with the beaten egg.

Make a small air vent in the top of each pasty, then cook in a preheated hot oven (200°C/400°F, Gas Mark 6) for 25 to 30 minutes until golden brown. Makes 4.

Potato and Lentil Goulash

Metric/Imperial	American
75 g/3 oz red lentils	⅓ cup red lentils
1 tablespoon oil	1 tablespoon oil
1 large onion, chopped	1 large onion, chopped
1×225 g/8 oz can tomatoes	1×8 oz can tomatoes
2 tablespoons tomato purée	2 tablespoons tomato paste
1 tablespoon Worcestershire sauce	1 tablespoon Worcestershire sauce
150 ml/¼ pint soured cream	⅔ cup sour cream
salt and pepper	salt and pepper
500 g/1 lb potatoes, boiled and thickly sliced	1 lb potatoes, boiled and thickly sliced
50 g/2 oz Cheddar cheese, grated	½ cup grated Cheddar cheese

Cook the lentils in simmering water for 30 minutes or until soft, then drain.

Heat the oil in a pan and sauté the onion until soft. Add the tomatoes with their juice, tomato purée (paste), Worcestershire sauce, soured cream, salt and pepper. Heat gently, stirring, for 1 minute.

Line the bottom of a greased 1.2 litre/2 pint (5 cup) ovenproof dish with potatoes, season with salt and pepper and cover with a layer of lentils. Arrange the remaining lentils and potatoes in layers, adding salt and pepper to each layer. Pour over the tomato mixture and sprinkle with the cheese. Cook in a preheated moderate oven (190°C/375°F, Gas Mark 5) for 30 to 40 minutes until golden. Serve hot with salad or green vegetables. Serves 4.

Wholewheat Vegetable Pancakes

Metric/Imperial	American
50 g/2 oz wholewheat flour	½ cup wholewheat flour
50 g/2 oz plain flour	½ cup all-purpose flour
pinch of salt	pinch of salt
1 egg	1 egg
300 ml/½ pint milk	1¼ cups milk
oil, for frying	oil, for frying
watercress, to garnish	watercress, for garnish
Filling:	*Filling:*
25 g/1 oz butter	2 tablespoons butter
250 g/8 oz celeriac, peeled and diced	½ lb celeriac, peeled and diced
350 g/12 oz leeks, sliced	¾ lb leeks, sliced
125 g/4 oz peas, cooked	¾ cup cooked peas
250 g/8 oz potatoes, boiled and diced	½ lb potatoes, boiled and diced
75 g/3 oz cream cheese with garlic and herbs	⅓ cup cream cheese with garlic and herbs
2-3 tablespoons milk	2-3 tablespoons milk
salt and pepper	salt and pepper
25 g/1 oz Cheddar cheese, grated	¼ cup grated Cheddar cheese
25 g/1 oz flaked almonds	¼ cup slivered almonds

Place the flours and salt in a bowl. Make a well in the centre and add the egg. Gradually add half the milk, mixing in the flour from the sides. Beat until smooth, then blend in the remaining milk. Pour the batter into a jug.

Heat an 18 cm/7 inch frying pan (skillet) and grease lightly with a little oil. Pour in enough batter to cover the bottom. Cook over a medium heat until golden brown underneath, then turn the pancake (crêpe) and cook the other side. Make 7 more pancakes (crêpes) in the same way. Keep warm in a folded tea towel or on a covered plate over a pan of simmering water.

To make the filling, heat the butter in a large pan and add the celeriac and leeks. Cover and sauté for 20 to 25 minutes until golden brown. Stir in the peas, potatoes, cream cheese and sufficient milk to moisten. Add salt and pepper to taste.

Divide the filling between the pancakes (crêpes) and roll up. Arrange in a greased shallow ovenproof dish. Sprinkle with the cheese and almonds, then cook in a preheated moderately hot oven (200°C/400°F, Gas Mark 6) for 15 minutes. Garnish with watercress and serve hot with wholewheat bread and salad. Serves 4.

Vegetable Crumble

Metric/Imperial	American
190 g/6½ oz wholewheat flour	1½ cups + 2 tablespoons wholewheat flour
125 g/4 oz butter	½ cup butter
75 g/3 oz Danish blue cheese, crumbled	¾ cup crumbled blue cheese
250 g/8 oz onions, sliced	½ lb onions, sliced
175 g/6 oz carrots, sliced	1¼ cups sliced carrots
4 celery sticks, chopped	4 stalks celery, chopped
3 teaspoons yeast extract	3 teaspoons brewers' yeast
450 ml/¾ pint boiling water	2 cups boiling water
350 g/12 oz potatoes, parboiled and chopped	¾ lb potatoes, parboiled and chopped
250 g/8 oz cabbage, finely shredded	3 cups finely shredded cabbage
250 g/8 oz tomatoes, skinned and sliced	½ lb tomatoes, peeled and sliced
salt and pepper	salt and pepper

Place 150 g/5 oz (1¼ cups) flour in a bowl and rub in half the butter until the mixture resembles fine breadcrumbs. Stir in the cheese.

Melt the remaining butter in a large frying pan and sauté the onions, carrots and celery for 10 minutes. Stir in the remaining flour and cook for 2 minutes.

Dissolve the yeast extract (brewers' yeast) in the boiling water and add to the pan. Heat, stirring, until thickened. Add the potatoes, cabbage, tomatoes and salt and pepper to taste.

Place the vegetables in an ovenproof dish and sprinkle the crumble over the top. Cook in a preheated moderate oven (180°C/350°F, Gas Mark 4) for 1 hour or until the topping is golden. Serve hot. Serves 4-6.

Vegetable Curry

Vegetable Curry

Metric/Imperial	*American*
2 tablespoons oil	2 tablespoons oil
1 onion, sliced	1 onion, sliced
1 tablespoon curry powder	1 tablespoon curry powder
1 teaspoon paprika	1 teaspoon paprika
2 teaspoons tomato purée	2 teaspoons tomato paste
1 teaspoon lemon juice	1 teaspoon lemon juice
1 tablespoon apricot jam	1 tablespoon apricot jam
300 ml/½ pint milk	1¼ cups milk
50 g/2 oz sultanas	⅓ cup golden raisins
1 kg/2 lb vegetables, e.g. potatoes, carrots, cauliflower, celery	2 lb vegetables, e.g. potatoes, carrots, cauliflower, celery
4 hard-boiled eggs, halved	4 hard-cooked eggs, halved
watercress sprigs	watercress sprigs

Heat the oil in a pan and sauté the onion for 5 minutes. Add the curry powder and paprika and continue to cook for 2 minutes. Stir in the tomato purée (paste), lemon juice, jam, milk and sultanas. Bring to the boil, lower the heat and simmer, uncovered, for 10 minutes.

Prepare the vegetables and parboil in salted water for 10 minutes. Drain well and add to the curry sauce. Continue simmering for 20 minutes or until the vegetables are tender. Transfer to a heated serving dish and garnish with the eggs and watercress. Serve with chutney and cucumber mixed with plain yogurt. This makes a substantial dish on its own or it can be served on a bed of brown rice.

Vegetable Casserole

Metric/Imperial	American
250 g/8 oz open mushrooms	½ lb open mushrooms
2 carrots, thinly sliced	2 carrots, thinly sliced
3 tomatoes, skinned	3 tomatoes, peeled
1 onion, sliced	1 onion, sliced
1 celery stick, chopped	1 stalk celery, chopped
1 × 425 g/15 oz can consommé soup	1 × 16 oz can consommé soup
750 g/1½ lb potatoes, boiled and mashed (see page 22)	1½ lb potatoes, boiled and mashed (see page 22)
salt and pepper	salt and pepper
wholewheat flour	wholewheat flour

Place half the mushrooms in a casserole and add the carrots, tomatoes, onion, celery and consommé. Cover and cook in a preheated moderately hot oven (190°C/375°F, Gas Mark 5) for 35 minutes.

Finely chop the remaining mushrooms and mix with the mashed potato, salt and pepper, and enough flour to give a firm consistency. Form into small cakes with floured hands and arrange around the top of the casserole. Return to the oven, uncovered, and continue to cook for 15 to 20 minutes until golden brown. Serve with a green salad. Serves 4.

Spinach Flan

Metric/Imperial	American
1 quantity Wholewheat Potato Pastry (see page 37)	1 quantity Wholewheat Potato Dough (see page 37)
500 g/1 lb spinach	1 lb spinach
salt and pepper	salt and pepper
grated nutmeg	grated nutmeg
2 eggs	2 eggs
150 ml/¼ pint milk	⅔ cup milk
125 g/4 oz Parmesan cheese, grated	1 cup grated Parmesan cheese

Roll out the pastry (dough) on a lightly floured surface and use to line a 20 cm/8 inch flan (pie) dish.

Place the spinach in a saucepan with a little water, cover and cook until soft. Drain throughly and mix with plenty of salt, pepper and nutmeg. Place the spinach in the flan case (pie shell).

Beat together the eggs, milk and cheese, add salt and pepper to taste, and pour over the spinach. Place the dish on a baking sheet and bake in a preheated moderately hot oven (190°C/375°F, Gas Mark 5) for 35 to 45 minutes until firm and golden. Serve hot or cold. Serves 4.

Nutty Baked Onions

Metric/Imperial	American
750 g/1½ lb onions, sliced	1½ lb onions, sliced
450 ml/¾ pint milk	2 cups milk
2 bay leaves	2 bay leaves
350 g/12 oz potatoes, parboiled and sliced	¾ lb potatoes, parboiled and sliced
40 g/1½ oz butter	3 tablespoons butter
40 g/1½ oz plain flour	6 tablespoons all-purpose flour
salt and pepper	salt and pepper
300 g/10 oz salted peanuts, chopped	2½ cups chopped salted peanuts
2 tablespoons chopped parsley, to garnish	2 tablespoons chopped parsley, for garnish

Place the onions in a pan with the milk and bay leaves. Bring to the boil, cover and simmer for 10 minutes. Drain, reserving the milk and discarding the bay leaves. Layer the onions and potatoes in a greased ovenproof dish.

Melt the butter in a pan, stir in the flour and cook for 1 minute. Remove from the heat and gradually blend in the reserved milk. Cook, stirring, until the sauce thickens. Continue to cook for 1 minute, then add salt and pepper to taste. Pour the sauce over the onions and potatoes and sprinkle the nuts over the top.

Bake in a preheated moderately hot oven (190°C/375°F, Gas Mark 5) for 20 to 30 minutes. If the nuts are browning too quickly, cover the dish with foil. Serve garnished with parsley. Serves 4.

Nut and Potato Croquettes

Metric/Imperial	American
500 g/1 lb potatoes, boiled and mashed (see page 22)	1 lb potatoes, boiled and mashed (see page 22)
15 g/½ oz butter	1 tablespoon butter
50 g/2 oz plain flour	½ cup all-purpose flour
oil, for frying	oil, for frying
1 small onion, finely chopped	1 small onion, grated
125 g/4 oz hazelnuts, chopped	1 cup chopped hazelnuts
1 teaspoon dried basil	1 teaspoon dried basil
salt and pepper	salt and pepper
dry breadcrumbs, to coat	dry bread crumbs, to coat
watercress, to garnish	watercress, for garnish

Mix the potatoes with the butter and flour. Heat 2 teaspoons oil in a small pan and sauté the onion until soft, then add to the potato with the hazelnuts and basil. Add salt and pepper to taste and mix well.

Divide the mixture into 8 and form each piece into a croquette. Roll each croquette in breadcrumbs, then fry in shallow or deep fat. Drain on kitchen paper towels, place on a warmed serving dish and garnish with watercress. Serves 4.

Mushroom and Pepper Pizza

Metric/Imperial	American
1 quantity Wholewheat Potato Pastry (see page 37)	1 quantity Wholewheat Potato Dough (see page 37)
2 tablespoons oil	2 tablespoons oil
250 g/8 oz onions, sliced	2 cups sliced onions
1 red pepper, cored, seeded and sliced	1 red pepper, seeded and sliced
1 green pepper, cored, seeded and sliced	1 green pepper, seeded and sliced
1 garlic clove, crushed	1 garlic clove, crushed
125 g/4 oz mushrooms, sliced	1 cup sliced mushrooms
salt and pepper	salt and pepper
125 g/4 oz Cheddar cheese, grated	1 cup grated Cheddar cheese
½ teaspoon oregano	½ teaspoon oregano

On a lightly floured surface, roll out the pastry (dough) to a 20 cm/8 inch round and carefully transfer to a large greased baking sheet.

Heat the oil in a pan and sauté the onions for 5 minutes. Reserve a few pepper rings for garnish, then roughly chop the remainder. Add to the onions with the garlic, mushrooms and salt and pepper and cook for a further 5 minutes.

Spread the mixture over the pastry (dough) base to within 1 cm/½ inch of the edge, cover with the cheese and arrange the pepper rings on top. Sprinkle with oregano and cook in a preheated hot oven (220°C/425°F, Gas Mark 7) for 35 to 40 minutes until the base is cooked and the cheese golden. Serve hot. Serves 4.

Variations

Tomato and Anchovy Sauté 3 sliced onions and sprinkle over the pastry round with 350 g/12 oz (2 cups) peeled and chopped tomatoes, ½ teaspoon oregano, salt and ground black pepper. Drain 1×50 g/2 oz can anchovies and arrange the fillets on top of the tomato mixture. Garnish with black olives, sprinkle with 125 g/4 oz (1 cup) grated cheese and bake as above.

Spinach and Ham Pizza

Sweetcorn and Tomato Drain 1×200 g/7 oz can sweetcorn (whole kernels) and mix the kernels with 1 teaspoon cornflour (cornstarch) and 150 ml/¼ pint (⅔ cup) soured cream. Spread over the pastry base and sprinkle with 75 g/3 oz (⅔ cup) grated Parmesan cheese, salt and ground black pepper. Garnish with 3 sliced tomatoes. Bake as above.

Spinach and Ham Sauté 1 chopped onion and 2 rashers (slices) chopped bacon in 1 tablespoon oil until soft. Add 50 g/2 oz (¼ cup) diced cooked ham and salt and pepper to taste. Arrange 250 g/8 oz (1 cup) cooked spinach over the pastry base and sprinkle ham mixture on top. Arrange 1 sliced tomato and 125 g/4 oz (¼ lb) sliced Mozzarella cheese on top of this. Sprinkle with ½ teaspoon dried oregano and bake as above.

Tuna Pizza Sauté 1 sliced onion in 1 tablespoon oil until soft then arrange on the pastry base. Flake 1×200 g/7 oz can tuna and sprinkle with 175 g/6 oz (1½ cups) grated Cheddar cheese. Sprinkle with salt and pepper and 1 tablespoon chopped parsley. Bake as above.

Potato Timbale

Metric/Imperial	American
1 kg/2 lb potatoes, boiled, mashed and sieved (see page 22)	2 lb potatoes, boiled, mashed and sieved (see page 22)
2 egg yolks	2 egg yolks
pinch of grated nutmeg	pinch of grated nutmeg
25 g/1 oz butter	2 tablespoons butter
500 g/1 lb cooked mixed vegetables (see below), roughly chopped	1 lb cooked mixed vegetables (see below), roughly chopped
4 hard-boiled eggs, sliced	4 hard-cooked eggs, sliced
parsley sprigs, to garnish	parsley sprigs, for garnish
Cheese sauce:	*Cheese sauce:*
15 g/½ oz margarine	1 tablespoon margarine
15 g/½ oz plain flour	2 tablespoons all-purpose flour
150 ml/¼ pint milk	⅔ cup milk
pinch of dry mustard	pinch of dry mustard
1-2 drops Worcestershire sauce	1-2 drops Worcestershire sauce
salt and pepper	salt and pepper
50 g/2 oz Cheddar cheese, grated	½ cup shredded Cheddar cheese

Beat together the potato, egg yolks, nutmeg and butter. Place three-quarters of the mixture in a piping (pastry) bag fitted with a large star nozzle and pipe a border around the edge of a 1.2 litre/2 pint (5 cup) pie dish.

To make the cheese sauce, melt the margarine in a pan, stir in the flour and cook for 1 minute.

Remove from the heat and gradually stir in the milk. Cook, stirring, over a gentle heat until the sauce thickens. Stir in the mustard, Worcestershire sauce, salt and pepper and continue to cook for 1 minute. Remove from the heat and stir in the cheese.

Arrange the vegetables and hard-boiled (-cooked) eggs in the pie dish and pour the sauce over. Pipe the remaining potato over the filling and place the dish under a preheated grill (broiler) for 5 minutes until golden. Serve immediately, garnish with parsley. Serves 4-6.

Note: Use a selection from the following: peas, beans, cauliflower, broccoli, mushrooms, carrots, Brussels sprouts, courgettes (zucchini).

Potato Nut Roast

Metric/Imperial	*American*
2 tablespoons oil	2 tablespoons oil
1 onion, chopped	1 onion, chopped
4 celery sticks, finely chopped	4 stalks celery, finely chopped
1 × 225 g/8 oz can tomatoes, drained and chopped	1 × 8 oz can tomatoes, drained and chopped
125 g/4 oz mushrooms, chopped	1 cup chopped mushrooms
250 g/8 oz mixed nuts, finely chopped	2 cups finely chopped mixed nuts
250 g/8 oz potatoes, boiled, mashed and sieved (see page 22)	½ lb potatoes, boiled, mashed and sieved (see page 22)
salt and pepper	salt and pepper
1 teaspoon Worcestershire sauce	1 teaspoon Worcestershire sauce
½ teaspoon dried or 1 teaspoon fresh basil	½ teaspoon dried or 1 teaspoon fresh basil
½ teaspoon ground coriander	½ teaspoon ground coriander
2 egg yolks	2 egg yolks

Heat the oil in a pan and sauté the onion and celery for 5 minutes. Add the tomatoes and mushrooms and continue to cook for 3 minutes.

Transfer the vegetables to a bowl and add the nuts and potatoes. Mix well, then stir in the salt and pepper, Worcestershire sauce, basil, coriander and egg yolks.

Blend the mixture thoroughly and spoon into a greased loaf tin (pan) measuring approximately 15×7.5×7.5 cm/ 6×3×3 inches. Cook in a moderately hot oven (200°C/ 400°F, Gas Mark 6) for 50 minutes to 1 hour until firm. Serve hot with vegetables and a cheese or tomato sauce, or cold with salad. Serves 4.

Potato Salads

Hot Potato Salad

Metric/Imperial	American
750 g/1½ lb new potatoes	1½ lb new potatoes
1 mint sprig	1 mint sprig
salt and pepper	salt and pepper
3 tablespoons oil	3 tablespoons oil
75 g/3 oz streaky bacon, rinds removed and chopped	5 fatty bacon slices, rinds removed and chopped
1 bunch spring onions, chopped	1 bunch scallions, chopped
1 tablespoon wine vinegar	1 tablespoon wine vinegar

Place the potatoes and mint in a pan and add enough boiling water to cover. Add a little salt, cover and simmer for 15 to 20 minutes until tender.

To make the dressing, heat the oil in a pan and cook the bacon for 5 minutes until crisp. Remove the pan from the heat and stir in the spring onions (scallions), vinegar, salt and pepper.

Drain the potatoes, removing the mint, and place in a serving dish. Pour over the hot dressing and serve immediately. Serves 4.

Sorrel, Egg and Potato Salad

Metric/Imperial	*American*
1 lettuce	1 head lettuce
250 g/8 oz new potatoes, boiled	½ lb new potatoes, boiled
4 tablespoons olive oil	¼ cup olive oil
4 hard-boiled eggs, sliced	4 hard-cooked eggs, sliced
4 tablespoons shredded sorrel	¼ cup shredded sorrel
salt and pepper	salt and pepper
½ teaspoon sugar	½ teaspoon sugar
½ teaspoon Dijon mustard	½ teaspoon Dijon-style mustard
1 tablespoon white wine vinegar	1 tablespoon white wine vinegar

Wash and dry the lettuce and arrange in a salad bowl. Slice the potatoes and pour 1 tablespoon olive oil over them while they are still warm. Pile into the centre of the lettuce and arrange the egg slices around the potato. Sprinkle the sorrel over the top. Make a dressing by mixing the remaining oil, salt and pepper, sugar, mustard and vinegar. Pour over the salad just before serving. Serves 4.

Chervil Potato Salad

Metric/Imperial	*American*
750 g/1½ lb new or waxy potatoes	1½ lb new or waxy potatoes
4 tablespoons thin cream	¼ cup light cream
150 ml/¼ pint homemade mayonnaise	⅔ cup homemade mayonnaise
sea salt and black pepper	sea salt and black pepper
3 tablespoons chopped chervil	3 tablespoons chopped chervil

Wash the potatoes and cook them in their skins in boiling salted water. As soon as they are cool enough to handle, skin them and slice thickly into a bowl. Stir the cream and mayonnaise into the warm potatoes. Add seasoning and the chervil. Serve warm. Serves 4-6.

Note: Use a fresh herb of your choice instead of chervil.

Hot Potato Salad

Granada Salad

Metric/Imperial	*American*
2 eggs, beaten	2 eggs, beaten
1 tablespoon milk	1 tablespoon milk
salt and pepper	salt and pepper
2 teaspoons oil	2 teaspoons oil
1 dessert apple	1 dessert apple
1 tablespoon lemon juice	1 tablespoon lemon juice
1 red pepper, cored, seeded and cut into strips	1 red pepper, seeded and cut into strips
350 g/12 oz potatoes, boiled and sliced	¾ lb potatoes, boiled and sliced
125 g/4 oz mushrooms, sliced	1 cup sliced mushrooms
75 g/3 oz stuffed green olives, sliced	½ cup sliced stuffed olives
1 lettuce	1 head lettuce
Dressing:	*Dressing:*
2 tablespoons olive oil	2 tablespoons olive oil
2 tablespoons dry sherry	2 tablespoons dry sherry
2 teaspoons Worcestershire sauce	2 teaspoons Worcestershire sauce
1 teaspoon caster sugar	1 teaspoon sugar
salt and pepper	salt and pepper
25 g/1 oz almonds, chopped	¼ cup chopped almonds

Beat together the eggs, milk, salt and pepper. Heat the oil in a frying pan (skillet), add the eggs and cook gently until set. Turn the omelette on to a plate, cool, and cut into squares.

To make the salad, core and slice the apple and toss in lemon juice. Arrange the pepper, potatoes, mushrooms, olives and lettuce leaves in a salad bowl and place the apple and omelette on top.

Mix together the oil, sherry, Worcestershire sauce, sugar, salt and pepper, and almonds. Pour over the salad and toss gently just before serving. Serves 4.

Variation

Use the segments from 1 orange instead of the apple.

Date and Walnut Salad

Metric/Imperial	American
250 g/8 oz new potatoes, boiled and diced	½ lb new potatoes, boiled and diced
2 dessert apples, cored and diced	2 dessert apples, cored and diced
2 teaspoons lemon juice	2 teaspoons lemon juice
75 g/3 oz dates, stoned and chopped	½ cup pitted chopped dates
50 g/2 oz walnuts, chopped	½ cup chopped walnuts
4 tablespoons mayonnaise	4 tablespoons mayonnaise
salt and pepper	salt and pepper

Place the potatoes in a bowl. Toss the apples in lemon juice and add to the potatoes with the dates, walnuts and mayonnaise. Toss well and add salt and pepper to taste. Chill before serving. Serve with cold meats or cheese, green salad and fresh bread. Serves 4.

Variation

Dieters can use natural yogurt instead of mayonnaise.

Peanut Potato Salad

Metric/Imperial	American
3 streaky bacon rashers, rinds removed	3 fatty bacon slices, rinds removed
500 g/1 lb new potatoes, boiled and diced	1 lb new potatoes, boiled and diced
3 tablespoons mayonnaise	3 tablespoons mayonnaise
1 tablespoon peanut butter	1 tablespoon peanut butter
lettuce leaves	lettuce leaves
50 g/2 oz salted peanuts	½ cup salted peanuts

Grill (broil) the bacon until crisp and dark brown, then chop into small pieces. Mix with the potatoes. Blend together the mayonnaise and peanut butter and mix into the potato and bacon. Arrange the lettuce leaves on a serving plate and spoon the potato mixture on top. Sprinkle with the peanuts. Serves 4.

Variation

Diced cooked ham can be used instead of bacon.

Vegetable Salad with Herb Sauce

Metric/Imperial	*American*
250 g/8 oz new potatoes, boiled	½ lb new potatoes, boiled
2 tablespoons olive oil	2 tablespoons olive oil
175 g/6 oz courgettes, sliced	1 cup sliced zucchini
175 g/6 oz French beans, sliced	1½ cups sliced green beans
1 bunch spring onions	1 bunch scallions
1 lettuce	1 head lettuce
Sauce:	*Sauce:*
2 hard-boiled eggs	2 hard-cooked eggs
2 tablespoons double cream	2 tablespoons heavy cream
2 tablespoons olive oil	2 tablespoons olive oil
2 teaspoons white wine vinegar	2 teaspoons white wine vinegar
salt and pepper	salt and pepper
1 tablespoon chopped chives	1 tablespoon chopped chives
1 tablespoon chopped dill	1 tablespoon chopped dill
1 tablespoon chopped tarragon	1 tablespoon chopped tarragon

Slice the potatoes while still warm and place in a bowl. Pour over 1 tablespoon olive oil and allow to cool.

Cook the courgettes (zucchini) in boiling salted water for 10 minutes, then drain, place in a bowl and sprinkle with 2 teaspoons olive oil. Cook the beans in boiling salted water for 10 minutes, then drain, place in a bowl and sprinkle with 2 teaspoons olive oil. Trim the spring onions (scallions), leaving the bulbs whole. Break the lettuce leaves into pieces and arrange in a salad bowl. Cover with the potatoes, courgettes, beans and spring onions.

To make the sauce, separate the yolks from the whites of the eggs. Chop the whites and sprinkle over the salad.

Mash the yolks and mix to a paste with the cream. Gradually blend in the olive oil, then stir in the vinegar. Add salt and pepper to taste, then stir in the chives, dill and tarragon. Pour over the salad and mix well. Serves 4.

Russian Salad

Metric/Imperial	American
500 g/1 lb potatoes, boiled and diced	1 lb potatoes, boiled and diced
125 g/4 oz carrots, cooked and sliced	¼ lb carrots, cooked and sliced
125 g/4 oz peas, cooked	¾ cup cooked peas
2 celery sticks, chopped	2 stalks celery, chopped
2 gherkins, chopped	2 gherkins, chopped
a few capers	a few capers
Dressing:	*Dressing:*
2 tablespoons vegetable oil	2 tablespoons vegetable oil
1 tablespoon wine vinegar	1 tablespoon wine vinegar
½ teaspoon sugar	½ teaspoon sugar
salt and pepper	salt and pepper
150 ml/¼ pint mayonnaise	⅔ cup mayonnaise

Place the potatoes in a bowl and add the carrots, peas, celery and gherkins.

Blend together the oil, vinegar, sugar, salt and pepper. Pour over the vegetables and toss well. Mix in the mayonnaise and transfer to a serving bowl. Sprinkle with the capers. Serve with cold meats. Serves 4-6.

Russian Salad

Greek Salad

Metric/Imperial	American
350 g/12 oz new potatoes, boiled and diced	3/4 lb new potatoes, boiled and diced
250 g/8 oz tomatoes, skinned, seeded and chopped	1/2 lb tomatoes, peeled, seeded and chopped
1 onion, finely chopped	1 onion, grated
50 g/2 oz black olives, stoned	1/3 cup pitted ripe olives
3 tablespoons mayonnaise	3 tablespoons mayonnaise
2 tablespoons milk	2 tablespoons milk
salt and pepper	salt and pepper

Place the potatoes in a bowl and add the tomatoes, onion and olives. Blend the mayonnaise with the milk and salt and pepper. Add to the vegetables and mix well. Transfer to a serving bowl and chill before serving. Serve with a mild creamy cheese and green salad. Serves 4.

Variation

For a main meal add 1 can tuna, flaked.

Chicken and Apple Salad

Metric/Imperial	American
300 g/10 oz cooked chicken, diced	1 cup diced cooked chicken
1 apple, cored and sliced	1 apple, cored and sliced
8 radishes, quartered	8 radishes, quartered
3 tablespoons mayonnaise	3 tablespoons mayonnaise
salt and pepper	salt and pepper
1 lettuce	1 head lettuce
250 g/8 oz small new potatoes, boiled	1/2 lb small new potatoes, boiled
mint, to garnish	mint, for garnish

Place the chicken, apple and radishes in a bowl. Add the mayonnaise and salt and pepper to taste. Mix well.

Arrange the lettuce leaves on a serving plate and pile the chicken mixture on top. Arrange the potatoes around the edge to form a border. Garnish with mint. Serves 4.

Prawn and Potato Salad

Metric/Imperial	American
500 g/1 lb new potatoes, boiled	1 lb new potatoes, boiled
2 celery sticks, chopped	2 stalks celery, chopped
½ cucumber, diced	½ cucumber, diced
2 teaspoons capers	2 teaspoons capers
250 g/8 oz peeled prawns	1½ cups shelled shrimp
150 ml/¼ pint mayonnaise	⅔ cup mayonnaise
salt and pepper	salt and pepper

Cut the potatoes into even-sized pieces and place in a bowl with the celery, cucumber, capers and prawns (shrimp). Add the mayonnaise and salt and pepper to taste. Toss well and transfer to a serving dish. Serves 4.

Egg and Potato Salad Loaf

Metric/Imperial	American
3 hard-boiled eggs, sliced	3 hard-cooked eggs, sliced
15 g/½ oz powdered gelatine	2 envelopes unflavored gelatin
2 tablespoons water	2 tablespoons water
3 tablespoons salad cream	3 tablespoons salad cream
1 teaspoon chopped chives	1 teaspoon chopped chives
1 small onion, grated	1 small onion, grated
salt and pepper	salt and pepper
750 g/1½ lb new potatoes, boiled and diced	1½ lb new potatoes, boiled and diced
shredded lettuce, to garnish	shredded lettuce, for garnish

Line a 1 kg/2 lb loaf tin (pan) with greaseproof (waxed) paper, letting it extend over the edges for about 5 cm/ 2 inches. Line the tin (pan) with slices of egg.

Sprinkle the gelatine over the water in a bowl. Place over a pan of gently simmering water until dissolved. Allow to cool and mix the gelatine with the salad cream, chives, onion, salt and pepper. Stir in the potatoes and spoon into the loaf tin (pan). Allow to set. Turn out and arrange shredded lettuce around the loaf. Serves 6.

Potato Soups

Pea and Potato Soup

Metric/Imperial	American
500 g/1 lb potatoes, boiled	1 lb potatoes, boiled
500 g/1 lb peas, cooked	3 cups cooked peas
600 ml/1 pint chicken stock	2½ cups chicken stock
1 teaspoon Worcestershire sauce	1 teaspoon Worcestershire sauce
1 × 170 g/6 oz can evaporated milk	1 × 6 oz can evaporated milk
salt and pepper	salt and pepper

Purée some of the potatoes and peas with a little of the stock in a blender or food processor. Continue until all the vegetables are puréed. Stir in the remaining stock, Worcestershire sauce, evaporated milk and salt and pepper to taste. To serve hot, heat and pour into warmed soup bowls. To serve cold, pour into bowls and chill. Garnish with chopped chives if liked. Serves 4.

Hearty Vegetable Soup

Metric/Imperial	American
50 g/2 oz pearl barley	⅓ cup pearl barley
1 large carrot, diced	1 large carrot, diced
1 large onion, sliced	1 large onion, sliced
1 leek, sliced	1 leek, sliced
1 small cauliflower, cut into florets	1 small cauliflower, cut into florets
350 g/12 oz potatoes, peeled and diced	¾ lb potatoes, peeled and diced
1.2 litres/2 pints chicken stock	5 cups chicken stock
salt and pepper	salt and pepper
125 g/4 oz frozen peas	¾ cup frozen peas

Place the pearl barley, carrot, onion, leek, cauliflower and potato in a large saucepan with the stock. Add salt and pepper, bring to the boil, cover and simmer for 1 to 1¼ hours until the barley is soft. Add the peas and cook for a further 15 minutes. Check the seasoning, then pour into a warmed soup tureen. Serve with hot baps. Serves 4.

Hearty Vegetable Soup

Watercress and Potato Soup

Metric/Imperial	American
25 g/1 oz butter	2 tablespoons butter
1 onion, chopped	1 onion, chopped
250 g/8 oz potatoes, peeled and chopped	1⅓ cups peeled and chopped potato
1 bunch watercress	1 bunch watercress
salt and pepper	salt and pepper
grated nutmeg	grated nutmeg
1.2 litres/2 pints chicken stock	5 cups chicken stock
5 tablespoons single cream	5 tablespoons light cream
watercress, to garnish	watercress, for garnish

Melt the butter in a saucepan and sauté the onion for 3 minutes. Add the potato, watercress, salt and pepper, nutmeg and stock. Bring to the boil, cover and simmer for 30 minutes or until tender. Purée a little at a time in a blender or food processor, or press through a sieve. Reheat and stir in the cream and pour into warmed soup bowls. Garnish with watercress. Serves 4-6.

Winter Soup with Sherry

Metric/Imperial	American
50 g/2 oz butter	¼ cup butter
250 g/8 oz swede, thinly shredded	½ lb rutabaga, thinly shredded
125 g/4 oz parsnip, diced	¼ lb parsnip, diced
125 g/4 oz potato, peeled and finely diced	¼ lb potato, peeled and diced
125 g/4 oz turnip, grated	¼ lb turnip, grated
¼ to ½ teaspoon ground turmeric	¼ to ½ teaspoon ground turmeric
1 teaspoon curry powder	1 teaspoon curry powder
1.2 litres/2 pints chicken stock	5 cups chicken stock
3 tablespoons sherry	3 tablespoons sherry
salt and pepper	salt and pepper
3 tablespoons chopped parsley	3 tablespoons chopped parsley

Melt the butter in a large saucepan. Add the swede (rutabaga), parsnip, potato and turnip, cover and sauté gently for 10 minutes or until beginning to soften.

Stir in the turmeric and curry powder, then pour in the stock. Bring to the boil, cover and simmer for 20 minutes or until the vegetables are soft. Stir in the sherry and add salt and pepper to taste. Pour into a warmed serving bowl and sprinkle with parsley. Serve with warm bread. Serves 6.

Parsley Soup

Metric/Imperial	American
50 g/2 oz butter	¼ cup butter
1 onion, sliced	1 onion, sliced
2 large carrots, sliced	2 large carrots, sliced
175 g/6 oz potato, peeled and diced	1 cup peeled and diced potato
900 ml/1½ pints chicken stock	3¾ cups chicken stock
salt and pepper	salt and pepper
25 g/1 oz parsley	¾ cup parsley
parsley, to garnish	parsley, for garnish

Heat the butter in a large saucepan and add the onion, carrots and potato. Sauté for 5 to 10 minutes until soft. Heat the stock in another pan and add to the vegetables. Add salt and pepper to taste, cover and simmer for 35 minutes or until the vegetables are tender.

Purée a little at a time with the parsley in a blender or food processor, or press through a sieve then add the parsley, finely chopped. Return to the rinsed-out pan and heat through. Check the seasoning and pour into warmed soup bowls. Garnish with parsley. Serves 4.

Leek and Potato Soup

Metric/Imperial	American
75 g/3 oz margarine	¼ cup + 2 tablespoons margarine
750 g/1½ lb leeks, sliced	1½ lb leeks, sliced
250 g/8 oz potatoes, peeled and diced	1⅓ cups peeled and diced potatoes
1 onion, chopped	1 onion, chopped
900 ml/1½ pints chicken stock	3¾ cups chicken stock
salt and pepper	salt and pepper
300 ml/½ pint milk	1¼ cups milk
2-3 tablespoons single cream	2-3 tablespoons light cream
chopped chives	chopped chives

Melt the margarine in a large saucepan and add the leeks. Sauté for 10 minutes, then add the potatoes and onion and cook for a further 5 minutes. Add the stock, salt and pepper, cover and simmer for 30 minutes or until the vegetables are soft.

Purée a little at a time in a blender or food processor, or press through a sieve. Return to the rinsed-out pan, add the milk and heat through gently. Check the seasoning and pour into warmed soup bowls. Swirl a little cream into each serving and sprinkle with chives. Serves 4.

Variation

Vichyssoise Make as above, but chill thoroughly when puréed. Before serving, stir in 150 ml/¼ pint (⅔ cup) milk and almost 150 ml/¼ pint (⅔ cup) single (light) cream, reserving a little to add to each serving.

Rösti

Rösti

Metric/Imperial	American
500 g/1 lb potatoes, boiled	1 lb potatoes, boiled
1 onion, finely chopped	1 onion, grated
salt and pepper	salt and pepper
50 g/2 oz unsalted butter	¼ cup unsalted butter

Chill the potatoes thoroughly, then grate into a bowl. Mix in the onion with salt and pepper to taste.

Melt half the butter in an 18 cm/7 inch frying pan (skillet) and add the potato mixture. Flatten with a palette knife and cook over a gentle heat until golden brown and crisp underneath. Slide on to a plate and invert on to another plate.

Melt the remaining butter in the pan (skillet), slide the Rösti into it with the uncooked side underneath and cook until the underside is golden and crisp. Turn on to a warmed serving plate and cut into wedges. Serve with roast or grilled (broiled) meats. Serves 4.

Potato and Green Pepper Ratatouille

Potato and Green Pepper Ratatouille

Metric/Imperial	American
2 tablespoons oil	2 tablespoons oil
250 g/8 oz potatoes, thinly sliced	½ lb potatoes, thinly sliced
1 onion, sliced	1 onion, sliced
2 green peppers, cored, seeded and sliced	2 green peppers, seeded and sliced
1 × 400 g/14 oz can tomatoes	1 × 16 oz can tomatoes
salt and pepper	salt and pepper
1 tablespoon soy sauce	1 tablespoon soy sauce

Heat the oil in a saucepan and sauté the potatoes, onion and peppers for 5 to 10 minutes. Add the tomatoes with their juice, salt and pepper and the soy sauce. Bring to the boil, cover and simmer for 40 minutes or until the vegetables are tender. Serve hot or cold as an appetizer or vegetable dish. Serves 4.

Gratin Dauphinois

Metric/Imperial	American
500 g/1 lb potatoes, thinly sliced	1 lb potatoes, thinly sliced
salt and pepper	sale and pepper
grated nutmeg	grated nutmeg
150 ml/¼ pint double cream	⅔ cup heavy cream
300 ml/½ pint milk	1¼ cups milk
25 g/1 oz butter	2 tablespoons butter
parsley to garnish	parsley for garnish

Arrange the potatoes in layers in a greased shallow oven-proof dish. Sprinkle each layer with generous amounts of salt, pepper and nutmeg. Stir half the cream into the milk and pour over the potatoes. Dot with butter and cook in a preheated moderate oven (180°C/350°F, Gas Mark 4) for 1¾ hours. Pour the remaining cream over and continue to cook for a further 20 minutes or until golden. Serve hot, sprinkled with parsley. Serves 4.

Potatoes Boulangère

Metric/Imperial	American
50 g/2 oz butter	¼ cup butter
1 kg/2 lb potatoes, peeled and sliced	2 lb potatoes, peeled and sliced
2 medium onions, sliced	2 medium onions, sliced
salt and pepper	salt and pepper
300 ml/½ pint chicken stock	1¼ cups chicken stock

Grease a 1.2 litre/2 pint (5 cup) ovenproof dish with 25 g/1 oz (2 tablespoons) butter. Arrange the potatoes and onions in alternate layers, adding plenty of salt and pepper between each layer. Finish with a neat layer of potato slices.

Pour over the stock, then dot with the remaining butter. Cover with a lid or foil and bake in a preheated moderate oven (160°C/325°F, Gas Mark 3) for 1½ to 2 hours until tender, removing the cover after 1 hour to allow the potatoes to brown. Serve hot. Serves 4-6.

Potatoes Anna

Metric/Imperial	American
750 g/1½ lb potatoes, peeled and thinly sliced	1½ lb potatoes, peeled and thinly sliced
salt and pepper	salt and pepper
125 g/4 oz butter	½ cup butter

Arrange the potatoes in layers in a greased shallow oven-proof dish. Sprinkle with generous amounts of salt and pepper between each layer.

Melt the butter and pour over the potatoes. Cover the dish with foil, place in a preheated moderately hot oven (190°C/375°F, Gas Mark 5) and bake for 30 minutes. Remove the foil and bake for a further 30 minutes or until the potatoes are tender and golden on top. Serves 4.

Potato and Parsley Stuffing

This is a delicious stuffing for chicken, duck, turkey or goose. To complete the meal, serve with Potato and Green Pepper Ratatouille (see page 87) or Rösti (see page 86) and green vegetables.

Metric/Imperial	American
15 g/½ oz beef dripping	1 tablespoon beef dripping
1 onion, finely chopped	1 onion, grated
250 g/8 oz pork sausage meat	1 cup pork sausage meat
250 g/8 oz potatoes, boiled and mashed	½ lb potatoes, boiled and mashed
salt and pepper	salt and pepper
8 tablespoons chopped parsley	8 tablespoons chopped parsley

Melt the dripping in a pan and sauté the onion for 3 minutes. Stir in the sausage meat and cook, stirring, until lightly browned. Remove from the heat and stir in the potato, salt and pepper and parsley. Use to stuff a large duck or chicken, as required.

Note: This recipe makes enough for a large duck or chicken. Double the quantity for a turkey or large goose.

Sweet Potato Cakes

Paradise Fingers

Metric/Imperial	American
1 quantity Basic Potato Pastry (see page 37)	1 quantity Basic Potato Pastry (see page 37)
3 tablespoons apricot jam	3 tablespoons apricot jam
125 g/4 oz butter	½ cup butter
125 g/4 oz caster sugar	½ cup sugar
1 egg	1 egg
50 g/2 oz mashed potato, sieved	¼ cup sieved mashed potato
25 g/1 oz ground almonds	¼ cup ground almonds
50 g/2 oz ground rice	⅓ cup ground rice
½ teaspoon almond essence	½ teaspoon almond extract
125 g/4 oz sultanas	⅔ cup golden raisins
50 g/2 oz glacé cherries, chopped	¼ cup chopped candied cherries
50 g/2 oz walnuts, chopped	½ cup chopped walnuts
caster sugar, to dredge	sugar, for dredging

Roll out the pastry (dough) on a floured surface and use to line a Swiss roll tin (jelly roll pan). Spread the jam over the bottom.

Cream the butter and sugar together until the mixture is pale and fluffy. Gradually beat in the egg and potato. Fold in the ground almonds, rice, almond essence (extract), sultanas (golden raisins), cherries and walnuts.

Spread the mixture over the jam and bake in a pre-heated moderate oven (180°C/350°F, Gas Mark 4) for 45 minutes or until firm and browned. Remove from the oven and sprinkle with sugar. Allow to cool in the tin (pan), then cut into fingers. Makes about 25.

Potato Gingerbread

Metric/Imperial	American
150 g/5 oz plain flour	1¼ cups all-purpose flour
1 teaspoon baking powder	1 teaspoon baking powder
1 teaspoon mixed spice	1 teaspoon mixed spice
1 teaspoon ground ginger	1 teaspoon ground ginger
pinch of salt	pinch of salt
75 g/3 oz potato, peeled and grated	½ cup peeled and grated potato
25 g/1 oz glacé cherries, chopped	1 tablespoon chopped candied cherries
50 g/2 oz sultanas	⅓ cup golden raisins
125 g/4 oz golden syrup	⅓ cup light corn syrup
50 g/2 oz butter	¼ cup butter
1 egg, beaten	1 egg, beaten
1 teaspoon bicarbonate of soda	1 teaspoon baking soda
1 tablespoon water	1 tablespoon water

Sift the flour, baking powder, spice, ginger and salt into a bowl. Stir in the potato, cherries and sultanas and mix well. Melt the syrup and butter in a small saucepan, allow to cool slightly, then add to the dry ingredients with the egg. Mix the soda with the water and add to the mixture. Beat well. Spoon into a greased and lined 23×13 cm/9×5 inch loaf tin (pan). Bake in a preheated moderate oven (180°C/350°F, Gas Mark 4) for 40 minutes or until the cake feels firm to touch. Makes 12-15 slices.

Paradise Fingers

Farmhouse Fruit Cake

Metric/Imperial	*American*
175 g/6 oz soft margarine	¾ cup margarine
175 g/6 oz demerara sugar	1 cup brown sugar
125 g/4 oz mashed potato, sieved	½ cup sieved mashed potato
1 tablespoon golden syrup	1 tablespoon light corn syrup
125 g/4 oz plain flour	1 cup all-purpose flour
125 g/4 oz wholewheat flour	1 cup wholewheat flour
3 teaspoons baking powder	3 teaspoons baking powder
1 teaspoon mixed spice	1 teaspoon mixed spice
3 eggs, beaten	3 eggs, beaten
125 g/4 oz sultanas	⅔ cup golden raisins
125 g/4 oz raisins	⅔ cup raisins
50 g/2 oz almonds, chopped	½ cup chopped almonds
50 g/2 oz glacé cherries, quartered	¼ cup quartered candied cherries
demerara sugar to top	brown sugar to top

Cream together the margarine and sugar until pale and fluffy, then beat in the potato and syrup. Mix together the flours, baking powder and mixed spice. Gradually beat the eggs into the creamed mixture, adding a little flour if necessary to prevent curdling.

Fold in the remaining flour with the sultanas (golden raisins), raisins, almonds and cherries. Spoon into a greased and lined 20 cm/8 inch deep cake tin (pan). Sprinkle the top with demerara (brown) sugar and bake in a preheated cool oven (150°C/300°F, Gas Mark 2) for 2½ hours or until risen and firm to touch. Leave in the tin for 5 minutes, then turn out on to a wire rack, remove the lining paper and allow to cool. Serve cut into wedges. Makes about 12 slices.

Helpful Hint

Potatoes can be mashed by hand using a ricer or potato masher but give the mixture a final beating with a wooden spoon. Alternatively mash the potatoes using an electric hand mixer or food processor.

Chocolate Cake

Metric/Imperial	American
125 g/4 oz margarine	½ cup margarine
175 g/6 oz caster sugar	¾ cup sugar
75 g/3 oz mashed potato, sieved	⅓ cup sieved mashed potato
40 g/1½ oz plain chocolate, melted	¼ cup melted semi-sweet chocolate
2 eggs, beaten	2 eggs, beaten
175 g/6 oz self-raising flour	1½ cups self-rising flour
½ teaspoon salt	½ teaspoon salt
4 tablespoons milk	4 tablespoons milk
grated chocolate, to decorate	grated chocolate, for decoration
Icing and filling:	*Frosting and filling:*
125 g/4 oz soft margarine	½ cup soft margarine
50 g/2 oz mashed potato, sieved	¼ cup sieved mashed potato
1 tablespoon cocoa powder	1 tablespoon unsweetened cocoa
300 g/10 oz icing sugar	2¼ cups confectioners' sugar

Cream the margarine and sugar together until pale and fluffy, then beat in the potato. Stir in the chocolate, then gradually beat in the eggs.

Sift the flour and salt together and fold into the mixture with the milk to make a soft dropping consistency.

Spoon into 2 greased and bottom-lined 20 cm/8 inch sandwich tins (layer cake pans). Bake in a preheated moderately hot oven (190°C/375°F, Gas Mark 5) for 25 to 30 minutes, until the cakes are firm and springy to touch. Turn out and allow to cool on a wire rack.

To make the icing (frosting), place the margarine and potato in a bowl and sift the cocoa and icing (confectioners') sugar over the top. Mix together until soft and smooth. Use half the icing (frosting) to sandwich the cakes together and half to cover the top. Decorate the top with grated chocolate. Makes about 12 slices.

Variation

Omit icing and use whipped cream to coat the cake.

Date and Nut Tealoaf

Date and Nut Tealoaf

Metric/Imperial	*American*
250 g/8 oz dates, stoned and roughly chopped	1 cup roughly chopped pitted dates
50 g/2 oz walnuts, chopped	½ cup chopped walnuts
25 g/1 oz margarine	2 tablespoons margarine
1 teaspoon bicarbonate of soda	1 teaspoon baking soda
125 g/4 oz demerara sugar	⅔ cup brown sugar
175 ml/6 fl oz boiling water	¾ cup boiling water
1 egg, beaten	1 egg, beaten
250 g/8 oz self-raising flour	2 cups self-rising flour
75 g/3 oz mashed potato, sieved	⅓ cup sieved mashed potato

Place the dates, walnuts, margarine, soda and sugar in a bowl. Pour over the boiling water, mix well and allow to cool. Stir in the egg, flour and potato and beat well with a wooden spoon. Spoon into a greased and lined 23×13 cm (9×5 inch) loaf tin (pan) and bake in a preheated moderate oven (180°C/350°F, Gas Mark 4) for 1 hour. Cover with foil and bake for a further 15 to 20 minutes until firm. Turn out and allow to cool on a wire rack. Serve sliced, with butter. Makes 12-15 slices.

Index

The publishers would like to acknowledge the following
photographers: Melvin Grey 2/3, 30, 35, 38, 87; Gina Harris 74;
Paul Kemp 7; Robert Golden 19, 27, 62, 71, 78, 86; and
Bryce Attwell 94.
Illustrations: Oriel Bath.
The publishers would also like to thank the following organisations
for their co-operation and photographs: Potato Marketing Board
50, 90; Mushroom Growers' Association 59; Egg Information
Bureau 15, 54; Sea Fish Industry Authority 46; Cadbury Typhoo
Limited 23; Canned Food Advisory Service; Dairy Produce
Advisory Service (Milk Marketing Board) 43, 66; and Knorr 82.